FIGHTER
AND STEALTH AIRCRAFT

Illustrations: Octavio Díez Cámara, Daimier-Benz Aerospace, Marta BAe Dynamics, British Aerospace, Eurofighter Jagdfluzeug Gmbh, Dassault Aviation, Saab-BAe Gripen AB, McDonnell Douglas Corporation, Military Industrial Group MAPO, Rosvoorouzhenie, Lockheed Martin-Boeling, Northrop Grumman Corporation, SRPC Zvezda-Strela, Hughes Aircraft, Texas Instruments Incorporated, Kongsber Gruppen ASA, Avibras Aeroespacial, US Navy, Pere Redón Trabal y Antonio Ros Pau.

Production: Ediciones Lema, S.L.
Editor: Josep M. Parramón Homs
Text: Octavio Díez
Co-ordination: Victoria Sánchez and Eduardo Hernández

I.S.B.N. 84-95323-15-X

Photocomposition and photomechanics: Novasis, S.A.L.
Barcelona (Spain)
Printed in Spain

ARMAMENT AND TECHNOLOGY

FIGHTER

AND STEALTH AIRCRAFT

LEMA
Publications

onceived as an advanced multi-purpose fighter bomber. The Eurofighter will make up the main combat element of the air forces of Germany, Spain, Italy and The United Kingdom.

Design Philosophy

It has been constructed using advanced materials including, from the beginning, an Integrated Logistic Support (ILS) system for its 15,000 components. 70% of its fuselage is made of carbon fiber composite materials, 15% is metal some of which are aluminium-lithium alloys, 12% is re-inforced plastic and 3% is made up of other materials.

To comply with ESR-D requirements the single and twin-seater versions (the latter maintaining full combat capability) of the Eurofighter were conceived as a supersonic twin-engine airplane with delta and canard wing configurations which make it an extremely agile and capable machine, carrying out combat maneuveres which were not possible in earlier models. Special emphasis has been put on the design of a low weight wing increasing its relationship with the thrust; a minimized radar signature; an ergonomic,

advanced cockpit which gives the pilot the possibility of excellent external vision; equipped with a sophisticated collection of systems for attack, identification and defence.

Advanced sensors

Among these a third generation ECR 90 multimode digital radar has been developed which evolves from the radar used to equip the Tornado ADV (Air Defence Variant) and that installed in the Sea Harrier F/A2, This radar has been produced by the Euroradar consortium made up of the British firm GEC Marconi, the Spanish ENOSA of the INDRA group, the Italian FIAR and the German Telefunken Systemtechnik. It is a Doppler system incorporating important technological advances with its arial, transmitter and signal processor. Complementing these is an

DEVELOPMENT CHRONOLOGY

YEARS	
• 1976	Independent Program Group raises the need for a new European combat airplane.
• 1980	CONTACTS ← France — DIFFERENCES — PROJECTS ← - ATC-92 Rafale 　　　　　　← Great Britain 　　　　　　← German Fed Rep — OWN — - EAP 　　　　　　　　　　　　　　　　　　　　　- TKF-90
• 1983	Incorporation of Italy and Spain
	Signing of OEST (Outline European Staff Target) Feasibility phase
• 1984	Signing of EST (Feasibility phase)
	Basic characteristics - 9.5 tons weight 　　　　　　　　　　　　2 jet engines with a unit thrust of 　　　　　　　　　　　　85 kilonewtons each
• 1985	Withdrawal of France
	Signing of ESR (European Staff Requirements): definition phase
• 1986	Creation of industrial consortiums - Eurofighter (aeronautical companies) 　　　　　　　　　　　　　　　　　　- Eurojet (engine companies)
• 1988	Signing of the development phase for the EFA prototype, jet engine and weapon systems.
• 1992	Reorientation of the program due to political reasons.
• 1994-1997	Flight of the prototypes - single-seater Germany 　　　　　　　　　　　　- DA2 Britain 　　　　　　　　　　　　- DA3 Italy 　　　　　　　　　　　　- DA7 Italy 　　　　　　　　　　　　- DA5 Germany 　　　　　　　　　　　　- Twin seater DA6 Spain 　　　　　　　　　　　　- Twin seater DA4 Britain: EJ 200 engine & ECR-90 radar

infra-red tracking and guidance system installed in the area in front of the cockpit on the left side, and complex electronic warfare equipment incorporated in the machine's own structure, identified by the abbreviation DASS (Defensive Aids Sub-System) and with the capability to give a reply, either automatically or manually, to multiple threats including a complete ESM/ECM system, various radar warning detectors, chaff and interference flare launchers.

At the same time it incorporates an avionics system which it optimizes as an element

MASS PRODUCTION

The delay in the budget authorization for the production of the Eurofighter in Germany meant its date for entering service was set back. However the budget for 1998 included the economic parts necessary to undertake the process of mass production (photograph above).

AGILE AND CAPABLE

Wings with a large surface area; quadrangular air inlet nozzles; flat canards to increase agility and an advanced cockpit design are some of the Eurofighter's characteristics, a machine which can compete with its French and United States counterparts (photograph below).

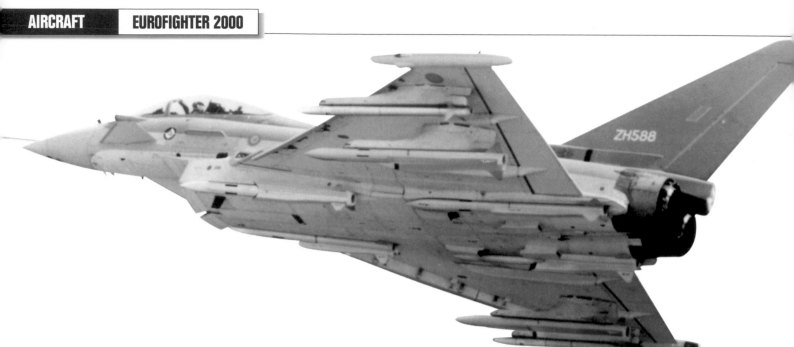

for aerial superiority and maintains additional capability for ground operations made up of seven functional sub-systems with a total of 24 computers linked together by data bases and optical fiber cables, all working together to supply the pilot with the maximum capability of managing tactical situations as well as flying. To improve this last aspect there is a Fly-By-Wire ACT (Active Control Technology) digital control system based on various computers which automatically control the aerodynamics against instability, giving

it the highest levels of agility.

This aspect is possible thanks to the incorporation of two EJ 200 jet engines which have been designed especially for this airplane and which have an improved reliability performance, along with reduced fuel consumption. Each one of these produces 14,000 pounds of thrust without re-heat and 20,000 when this is employed, controlled by a digital system which opti-

---

A FIGHTER PLANE ABOVE ALL

Conceived mainly to carry out air to air missions its weaponry can include an internal cannon, six short range infra-red missiles and six medium range laser guided missiles. At the same time it can carry out air to surface missions against land or naval targets.

RADAR SIGNATURE

The large quadrangular nozzles below the cockpit have needed intensive work to reduce the machine's radar signature as much as possible, although in this aspect its characteristics don't seem to be noteworthy.

---

mizes its operation in whatever functional state.

Advanced cockpit

The cockpit incorporates a MK16A Martin Baker ejectable seat and facing the pilot there are three large color MHDD's (Multi-Function Head Down Displays), usually including data on the tactical situation, information on the state of the various sub-systems and maps of the terrain combined with the positions of aerial traffic. There is also a HUD (Head Up Display) visor with the responsibility of supplying basic flight data so that the pilot does not have to look inside the airplane for the information. This is complemented by the display system which is incorporated in the flight helmet using the HMS (Helmet Mounted Symbology) system, where the helmet incorporates a night vision facility and protection against various optical threats.

The VTAS (Voice Throttle And Stick) system allows the pilot to easily carry out complex missions in extremely intense situations. The joystick allows more than twenty functions to be carried out with respect to the control of sensors, weapons, the management of defence systems and flight handling, whereas the DVI (Direct Voice Input) system can be used to change presentation mode from HUD to

MHDD, select targets and radio frequencies, all of these functional changes carried out by voice.

Weaponry Capacity

There are a total of thirteen fixing points (excluding the three for attaching additional fuel), with four on each of the wings and five on the fuselage, allowing the loading of different weapons up to a maximum of 6.5 tons. In air-to-air missions it can carry up to six radar-guided medium range missiles-AMRAAM (Advanced Medium Range Air-to-Air Missiles) positioned on the fuselage or in sub-wing mountings; six short range infra-red guided missiles-ASRAAM (Advanced Small Range Air to Air Missile) in sub-wing mountings; a 27mm Mauser cannon incorporated in the fuselage; it can employ older missiles such as Sidewinder, Sparrow, Aspide etc. For air-to-surface missions there are seven fixing points for locating free fall bombs, guided bombs, air-to-surface & anti-ship missiles, laser designators and various assemblies of associated equipment.

Its capability, reliability and multi-purpose nature make this a very advanced air-plane for which reason the air forces of Australia, The Arab Emirates, and Norway have expressed their interest, meaning in the medium term a large number of export possibilities are foreseen.

TECHNICAL CHARACTERISTICS

COST:	72 million dollars		**Internal fuel**	4,000 kilograms
DIMENSIONS:			**External fuel**	4,500 kilograms
Length	15.96 metres		**PROPULSION:**	
Height	5.28		2 Eurojet EJ 200 jet engines of 9,000kg thrust each.	
Wingspan including missile launchers	10.95m		**PERFORMANCE:**	
Wing surface area	50m²		Service ceiling height	15,000 metres
canards surface area	2.4m²		Speed at high altitude	Mach 2
WEIGHTS:			Speed at low altitude	Mach 1
Empty	9.999 kilograms		Runway take off length	700 metres
Maximum	21,000 kilograms		Interception range	600 kilometres
Maximum ext. load	6,500 kilograms		Extended range	3,000 kilometres
			Design factor	9g

INFRA-RED SENSOR

These models have an infra-red sensor located in the front left part of the cockpit, which improves the possibilities of its use in any weather conditions.

MULTIFUNCTIONAL RADAR

The ECR-90 multifunctional digital radar has been designed as a component with high operational readiness, with improved reliability and requires minimum maintenance. Its transmission power allows it to continue detecting aircraft at distances of hundreds of kilometres even when the atmosphere is being saturated by electronic counter-measure equipment, and it is capable of discerning the potential of distinct threats facing it.

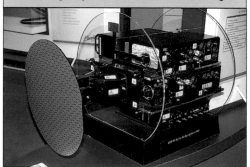

LOWER AIR INTAKE

The fuselage has a quadrangular lower section due to the design of the large air intakes for the jet engines. This characteristic improves its functionality in some aspects of use and at the same time facilitates the positioning of medium-range missiles along its sides. The forward landing gear folds back between the entrance for the lower nozzles.

OPTIMIZED CANARDS

At both sides of the cockpit two large canards have been positioned, controlled by the on board digital computer to optimize the aircraft's capability to maneuvere at any flight altitude. A greater angle of attack, reduced turning radius, improved flight control with increased loads and greater lift are some of the parameters which define the canard's qualities.

OPTIMIZED COCKPIT

The cockpit incorporates a MK16A Martin Baker seat which guarantees ejection at any altitude; there are three large color MHDD's (Multi-Function Head Down Displays) in which all the parameters necessary for the mission can be visualized; a HUD visor (Head Up Display) which presents data to the pilot while he is visualizing the tactical situation and the VTAS (Voice Throttle And Stick), combining all the elements for total control of the aircraft.

TAIL RUDDER

The tail rudder, with its large cross sectional area, presents some advantages when carrying out missions needing combat agility and attack capability.

AUXILIARY INTAKE

Air is channeled to a dynamic refrigeration system for many of the electronic systems, which are kept inside the fuselage.

ADVANCED ELECTRONIC WAR

The housings located on the peripheral edges of the wings contain sophisticated electronic war systems (DASS).

PROPULSION UNITS

Reduced fuel consumption, increased operational capability, increased power as much with post-combustion as without it, and a thrust to weight ratio of 10 to 1. These are some of the characteristics which define the EJ 200 engines. Of modular construction it incorporates advanced components and digital control which optimizes its functioning at any altitude and mode of employment.

WEAPONRY

Close to six and a half tons of arms can be located on the five fixing points on the fuselage and on the four on the wings. On three of these it is possible to locate auxiliary fuel tanks which increase the range of movement as much as the combat range. Short-range missiles, medium-range missiles, free fall and guided bombs, air-to-surface missiles, sub-munitions magazines, stand-off weapons, equipment housings etc, can be carried to enable the carrying out of any mission assigned.

Late in the afternoon of the 7th June 1981, eight airplanes left the Sinai from their Etzion base loaded with 907 kg Mk84 bombs. Flying close to the ground so as not to be picked up by radar, they crossed the 960 kilometers which separated them from Iraq's nuclear power station at Osirak, launching their bombs with precision onto the thick concrete walls and destroying the station completely. This combat mission, which was widely reported by the international press, was executed by Israeli F-16s.

Originally conceived as an aircraft which was easy to operate, economic and with some advanced features inherent in the original design, the General Dynamics F-16 has achieved notable sales success with some 4,000 units in service in nearly twenty countries.

MULTINATIONAL
Bought as a part of the Multinational program to equip four NATO countries, the Belgian F-16s make up the main offensive-defensive element of its airforce (photograph to the right).

SERVICE
Apart from forming part of the machinery of the Reserve and National Guard Airforces in addition to the air potential of a further sixteen countries, the F-16 has demonstrated that a well equipped lightweight fighter can carry out, without problem, air-to-air and air-to-surface missions (photograph below).

A light weight fighter

Its development originated from the LWF (Light Weight Fighter) program of the United States Air Force, which advocated the construction of a simple daytime fighter of aerial superiority, light and economical which could complement the more

sophisticated F-15. In this way a prototype YF-16 was constructed which had its first flight on the 2nd of February 1974.

The selection

On the 13th of January 1975 the choice was announced and so began a process of engineering development on a grand scale which allowed it to meet all the initial requirements as well as other later ones which, proposed the installation of a radar, and the capability to attack surface objects.

8 pre-production units were contracted, 6 F-16A single-seater and 2 F-16B twin-seaters. The first of which flew on the 8th of December 1976, and the last on the 8th of June 1978 carrying out all of the evaluations at Edwards Air Force Base, California. In parallel Belgium, Denmark, the Netherlands, and Norway decided to adopt it and began manufacturing under license.

The production phases

Production of the A model began in the Spring of 1978 and the most important user has been the United States with 2,300 aircraft shared among the units of the USAF, the Reserve & National Guard with some hundreds stockpiled in a state of operational readiness over a long period of time. The first United States unit entered service in January 1979 in 338 TFW at the Hill Air Force Base in Utah, with production continuing in blocks of 1, 5, 19 & 15 until March 1985. Later they were modernised and incorporated the OCU (Operational Capabilities Upgrade) applied to the 15 block in 1987.

The C version entered production in 1984 in the 25 block and benefited from

ADVANCED

The «Halcon Volador» is provided with the new Northrop-Grunman AN/APG-68 radar which permits the detection of other aircraft, guided missiles or for it to follow the ground. These among another 25 modes of operation in which it can operate allow this multipurpose aircraft to execute the most varied of combat missions (photograph below).

OPERATION

Its low operational requirements with respect to maintenance and the ease of locating break-down problems through specific purpose panels facilitate its use in any part of the world (photograph to the left).

the second phase of the MSIP (Multinational Stage Improvement Program) upgrades, which in parallel introduced substantial changes to the cockpit and aircraft structure. The third phase of MSIP was begun shortly after this. Deliveries of 30/32 blocks began in July 1986, these were different in that the first employed a General Electric F110-GE-100 jet engine and the second a Pratt & Whitney F100-PW-220. They were modernized between 1986 & 1992 with nearly three hundred units in the National Guard under the premises of the ADF program this gives them the capability to use medium-range guided missiles.

The delivery of the 40/42 block began in December 1988, and in 1990 three hundred were modified to carry out CAS/BAI missions. Improvements to the engines were carried out from 1991 to a variety of

different versions, and in May 1991 the MLU (Mid Life Update) was approved and applied to 300 units of the USAF and to aircraft of the NATO consortium up to 1999. In October 1991 the 50/52 block was delivered and from May 1993 these have been given the capability to launch «Harm» anti-radar missiles, going on to be called the 50D/52D. In 1993 the ground training GF-16A was accepted by the 82 Training Wing at Sheppard Air Force Base.

DEPLOYMENT

The possibility of refuelling in flight and its wide radius of action allows it to be deployed from any kind of operational base.

combination of its advanced features and great potential in air-to-air or air-to-surface combat inherent in its original design.

The cockpit
The cockpit is notable for its design incorporating a Head Up Display (HUD) and multi-functionary screens, which present the data from the Westinghouse AN/APG-66 or the Northrop-Grumman AN/APG-68 (v) doppler radar which locates arial targets and locks the missiles on to it. In secondary missions this also includes tracking terrain.

The canopy is made out of one polycarbonate piece with a fine gold film applied this helps to dissipate radar transmissions, with the result that the aircrafts front radar signature is reduced by 40%, and providing the pilot an exceptional field of view. The McDonnel Douglas ACES II ejection seat is reclined at an angle of 30 degrees to improve the tolerance of the crew to increased gravity loadings- g's, which are

WEAPONRY

AIR TO AIR MISSIONS	AIR TO SURFACE MISSIONS
- 20mm multi-barrelled cannon from General Electric, type M61A1 Vulcan, with a magazine of 511 rounds	
- short-range infra-red missiles:	- Free fall & laser guided
«Sidewinder» AIM-9 and «Magic»	bombs
- medium range guided missiles:	- CGPU 5/A
«Sparrow» AIM-7 & AIM-120	Housings with 30mm cannons milímetros
«AMRAAM»	- «Maverik» AGM-65 missiles
	- «Harm» anti-rradar missiles
	- «Harpoon» anti-ship missiles
	«Penguin» Mk3

Forty were modified and given the designation QRC (Quick Reaction Capability) and towards the end of 1995 went into operation in the skies above Bosnia.

INTERCEPTOR

Equipped with up to four AIM-120 «AMRAAM» medium-range guided missiles, or supplied with short-range AIM-9 «Sidewinder» infra-red missiles, this lightweight fighter constitutes the basic elements of hunting and intercepting other aircraft, and further, is noteworthy for its agility and combat capability.

An outstanding airplane

The notable sales success is due to the

pulled during maneuveres. The joystick is located on the right side to facilitate the control of the aircraft while the pilot is paying attention to what is happening around him-ie the HOTAS concept (Hand On Throttle And Stick). This keeps the arm in a comfortable position while carrying out the mission. A four channel ditital flight control of the "fly-by-wire type" allows maneuveres to be executed with precision and speed.

Its design

With the wings incorporated into the fuselage, the aircraft has a robust and light-weight structure. This has allowed the fuel capacity to be increased while at the same time its support ability has been improved with increased angles of attack. The wing layout also incorporates two large flaps below the stern side of the fuselage, mounted at an oblique angle with the function of giving directional stability in extreme wind conditions.

With only one engine either the Pratt & Whitney F100-PW-220 or General Electric F110-GE-100. It is flown with great agility and fed through a single fixed-air intake

ANTI-SHIP

In accordance with the requirements of Norwegian specifications, the anti-ship missile «Penguin» Mk3 has been incorporated in the F-16, and with an operational range of 55 kilometers it can attack medium sized ships thanks to an explosive load of 140 kilograms. This gives an increased capability to this fighter bomber.

below the dividing plate under the fuselage. This positioning ensures the flow of fuel to the engine at elevated angles of attack, although it has the inconvenience of taking in foreign objects when operating from unprepared runways. Nevertheless it is utilized to house the robust three-piece landing gear, with the two main rear carriages going forward & up, and the front carriage pulled back and up.

TWINSEATER

With a similar capability to the single-seater the F-16B can carry out pilot training work in addition to combat missions.

C VERSION CHARACTERISTICS

COST:	22 million dollars			to 2.567 kg for
DIMENSIONS:				the D single seater
Length	15.03 m		**External fuel**	3.066 kg
Height	5.09 m		**PROPULSION:**	
Wingspan including			A Pratt & Whitney F100-PW-220 jet engine with 13,000 kilograms	
Missile launchers	9.45 m		thrust or a General Electric F100-GE-100 with 10,770 kg.	
Wing surface area	27.87 m²		An improved version with greater power has also been	
Flap surface area	2.91 m²		introduced , designated 100-PW-229 and F110-GE-129.	
WEIGHTS:			**PERFORMANCE:**	
Empty	8,273 kg with		Service ceiling height	15,240m
	F100-PW-220		High altitude speed	Mach 2
	engine and 8.627 kg		Low altitude speed	Mach 1
	with F100-GE-100 engine.		Runway length	360 m
Maximum 40/42 block	19,187 kg		Interceptor range	1,315 km
Maximum external load	5,443 kg		Extended range	3,890 km
Internal fuel	3,104 kg reduced		Design factor	9g

RADAR HOUSING

Housing the Westinghouse AN/APG-66 doppler radar dish or the more advanced Northrop-Grumman AN/APG-68, depending on the aircraft's year of manufacture giving complete capability for the tracking of various targets in air-to-air combat and missile guidance.

AIR INTAKE

Its design and positioning in a very low position allows the entry of the required airflow to guarantee the correct functioning of the engine at whatever speed and height, although there is the inconvenience of its position facilitating the intake of foreign objects during take-off.

LANDING CARRIAGE

Originally designed as a light weight and economic fighter, it was given a simple, but robust landing carriage. Its front undercarriage is located just under the large engine air intake with a small directional wheel which folds back and up , rotating 90 degrees in the process. The rear carriage is somewhat stronger.

COCKPIT

Provided with a polycarbonate canopy which gives the pilot good visibility, the cockpit has an angled ejectable seat improving resistance to the effects of gravitational pull and equipment which gives it the possibility to carry out multiple missions. A noteworthy part of this equipment is the Head Up Display (HUD) which appears in front of the pilot.

TAIL

UHF/IFF antennas are located on the front edge and on the upper part is the VHF antenna for high frequency communication. There is also a powerful rotating flashing light which acts as a beacon to avoid accidents.

NOZZLE

Below the tail, which includes electronic counter measure equipment and an auxiliary parachute for braking, there is a unique, high performance jet engine which delivers the power necessary for carrying out missions.

ALL WEATHER OPERATION

Housings with infra-red tracking equipment are attached to the underside of the fuselage allowing it to carry out air-to surface missions with precision day and night, increasing its utilization possibilities.

CAPABILITY

The rails at the wing edges, the sub-wing supports and the fuselage fixings all allow the transportation of a wide range of equipment including launchable weapons, fuel tanks, or housing to carry auxiliary equipment.

onceived for use on large United States aircraft carriers, the Grumman F-14 naval fighter is notable for a satisfactory combination of agility, acceleration, speed and range together with the capability for using a wide range of weapons in short, medium & long range air-to-air missions. All of which make it one of the best fighter planes at the present time. It is predicted that this model will continue in operational service until at least the year 2010.

It is famous for its intervention in aerial combat against Libyan Sukhoi aircraft in the Sirte Gulf, which were shot down with relative ease, and also for being the primary aircraft used in the «Top Gun» school, improving the ability of United States naval pilots. The «Tomcat» commands respect from its opponents for its capability and performance.

A highly developed model

After the failure in the development of a naval fighter craft TFX (Tactical Fighter Experimental), the United States Navy, towards the end of 1967, decided to build

LATEST MODEL

The F-140 D «Tomcat» is the most advanced of the United States naval-fighters, incorporating notable technological advances which will allow it to carry out interception and attack roles until the end of the first decade of the 21st century.

NAVAL INTERCEPTOR

Conceived with the idea of being used on large United States aircraft carriers the F-14 has demonstrated its potential for twenty five years and it is expected to be in active service until the end of the next decade.

an interceptor for the fleet, giving it the abbreviation VFX.

The decision

Once the qualities of the Grumman 303-60 were tested out and various modifications made, it was chosen as the winning aircraft and identified as the F-14 «Tomcat». Charged with the construction of 12 development models, the first prototype began its trials in Calverton on the 14th of December 1970.

The construction of 497 units was undertaken, the first F-14s of the series being delivered to the NAS Miramar VF-124

as «Bobcat» this improvement is based on the substantial modifications made to the weapons operator's display screen, and with the introduction of a variety of equipment including the LANTIRN (Low Altitude Navigation and Targeting Infra-Red, Night) and the IRST (Infra-red, Search and Track).

«Super Tomcat»

Between the 23rd of March 1990 and the 20th of July 1992 thirty seven new F-14D «Super Tomcats» were received with the capability of employing new missiles, night system compatible cockpits, advanced tactical display systems and the AN/APG-71 radar, having undertaken the modifications of 18 older units of this version. In parallel, modifications to other aircraft have been taking place to allow them to carry a reconnaissance pod called TARPS (Tactical Air Reconnaissance Pod) from a central hook up point. With this they are able to collect and send in real time digitalized images through a coded radio communication system, to any ship or ground position which uses the system Link 11.

In future it is expected that the fleet will incorporate the satellite positioning sys-

«Gunfighters» squadron. In 1973 a squadron boarded the U.S.S. «Enterprise» for operational assessment, some of these covered the evacuation of Saigon during the operation «Frequent Wind». The total number of units produced was 557, production ended in April 1987. A batch of 79 aircraft was destined for Iran of which twenty are maintained in operational condition, which were imposed, after the sanctions.

Modernization of the F-14

A few months before the end of production the first flight of the B version had taken place with improved avionics and propulsion, using the F110-GE-400 engine from General Electric. After initial trials the production of 38 new aircraft began. The first of which was received on the 11th of April 1988, and the last in May 1990, at the same time as the modification of some A types to a version originally designated as A plus, which was finally known as B.

This process continued until a short time ago, although Northrop Grunman has been involved in the supply of different equipment which allows the installation of additional capability to make precision attacks. Known

tem GPS (Global Positioning System), communication equipment from the AN/ARC-210 family, AN/ALE-50 interference systems, advanced mission recorders and digital flight control systems, among others.

A naval fighter

With a squadron of 14 «Tomcats» assigned to each United States aircraft carrier to supply the means of establishing combat air patrols (CAP) and making up the long range interception force, the F-14 is still considered to be a highly powerful fighter aircraft. 750 units have been manufactured of which 323 remain in service with others stored in a position of long term operational capability at Mountain Home air base in Arizona. A process which has required

INTERCEPTOR
With six AIM-54 « Phoenix» long range missiles located in the sub-wing and fuselage fixing points the F-14B carries out its missions in an interception zone with the objective of destroying any aerial target which comes within 200 kilometers of the established combat patrol area.

LANTIRN
Navigation and tracking equipment is carried in a pod fixed below the fuselage, allowing the destruction of surface targets in any weather conditions (photograph to the left).

POTENTIAL
With modernized avionics such as AN/ALQ-165 ASJP self protection equipment, the F-14D still constitutes a naval fighter of some note, with enough power to face up to later designs (photograph to the right).

external sealing and partial covering with a protective material.

An advanced design

The possibility of varying the angle of the external sections of the wings enhances its suitability for its role as an interceptor. The "arrow" can be adjusted between 20 and 68 degrees improving its aerodynamic efficiency and varying its lift. For naval use it has a robust undercarriage with a launch bar in the front wheel, a braking hook that catches a cable during landing and a nozzle which allows it to receive fuel during flight.

Located in the rear part just below the two large tail planes and the hydraulic air brake, we find the two F110-GE-400 General Electric engines which supply a total of 24,260 kgs of thrust, thus there is

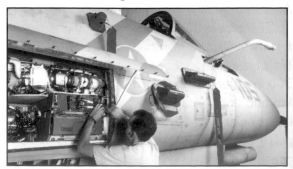

D MODEL CHARACTERISTICS

COST:	58 million dollars			Internal fuel	7,348 kg
DIMENSIONS:				External fuel	1,724 kg
Length	19.1 m		PROPULSION:	TWO GENERAL ELECTRIC F110-GE TURBOFANS WITH 12,230 KG OF THRUST EACH.	
Height	4.88 m		PERFORMANCE:		
Wingspan with wings extended	19.54 m		Service ceiling height		16,650 m
Wingspan with wings retracted	11.65 m		Speed at high altitude		Mach 1.88
Wing surface area	52.49 m²		Speed at low altitude		Mach 0.72
WEIGHTS:			Interception range		800 km
Empty	18,951 kg		Extended range		2,965 km
Maximum	33,724 kg		Design load factor		+7.5 g
External max load	6,577 kg				

more power, less fuel consumption, and better reliability than the originals, although they are still a little short on power.

Shared tasks

With an advanced capability for the time in which it was conceived, the cockpit combines various controls along the sides and analogue and digital gauges in front. Among the latter there is a Head Up Display HUD, a large display screen (Vertical Display Indicator) and a maneuveres control panel and in the pilot's hands a joystick which is moved in the conventional way.

For his part the co-pilot, who is given the designation RIO (Radio Intercept Officer), has at his disposition a large circular display (Tactical Situations Display) which allows him to see all the relevant information on the different radar screens, this offers a detailed picture of the tactical situation with the most serious threats being brought to his attention. There are various weapon control panels he can use; communication and IFF identification equipment; electronic war system; navigation data displays; fuel gauges.

ADVANCED

The capabilities of the «Tomcat» as a interceptor are due to the combination of advanced design and sophisticated equipment, which make it the most capable of its kind.

Avionics

The oldest «Tomcats» rely on the powerful AN/AWG-9 Hughes radar which is capable of detecting targets at distances of up to 300 kilometers, to lock onto this data at 24 km and enter combat at 6 km. However, the latest units built have an AN/APG-71 monopulse with greater processing capacity which presents greater reliability and emission

TWIN SEATER

The cockpit of the F-14 was designed for two operators with the responsibility of handling the aircraft as well as the weapon control systems, for which each position was designed with the equipment necessary for the task.

power. The power of the radar gives it the capability to be employed as a limited aerial warning alert system (AWACS), a task which the Iranian units still in service have been carrying out, despite the maintenance difficulties.

Along with this radar system there is the AN/ AWG-15F Fairchild Fire Control System; various data processing computers; the AN/ASW-27B digital coded communication link; the AN/AXX-1 television system TCS (Television Camera Set) and the IRST sensor located in the small housing inside the cone which covers the radar. AN/ ALE-29 Goodyear launchers- 39 for decoy flares; the AN/ALQ-100/126/165 ASPJ eletronic deception system.

The weaponry of the F-14
All aircraft carry a General Electric M6

1A1 20mm cannon and a variable combination of missiles which can include four short range infra-red AIM-9 «Sidewinders», four me-dium-range radar guided AIM-7 «Sparrows», six long-range AIM-54C+ «Phoe-nixs». The latter is capable of intercepting targets with a 150 kilometer radius thanks to a design which combines its long range capability with an independent tracker which is able to distinguish between real echos and earlier ones coming from a variety of interference equipment.

Additionally some units, known as «Bobcat», have been modified to carry out attack missions in which different types of weapons can be employed including Rockeye & CBU-59 Cluster bombs, Gators & CBU-16 laser guided bombs, AGM-88 «Harm» anti-radar missiles with the possibility that they will be given the capability of launching «SLAM» missiles, a variant of the «Harpoon» anti-ship missile designed to reach armored targets located in enemy territory.

STRENGTHENED LANDING CARRIAGE
Take offs and landings on aircraft carriers demand that the landing gear is strengthened with the capability of coping with the enormous strain involved in this activity (photograph to the right).

PROPULSION
Despite the aircraft being of considerable weight the two General Electric F110-GE-400 turbofans transmit the power necessary to carry out attack and interception missions (photograph above).

DESIGN
Despite a design dating back to the 1970s the beauty of the Tomcat lines is undeniable, designed to give the best performance and speed in its basic role as a naval interceptor with the fleet, it is also an aircraft used in other kinds of missions.

The political, economic and military independence shown by Sweden in the last century and a capacity for self sufficency in matters of security. Have enabled it to develop an advanced and competitive industry which in the aeronautical area, it has been able to design the SAAB 35 «Draken» as well as different models of the Saab 37 «Viggen».

The necessity to face up to the challenges of the 21st century was the motivation for beginning this ambitious program, with the main objective of deseigning an advanced multi-purpose fighter which could complement the «Viggen» and enjoy the highest level of quality and capability.

MANOEUVRES
In flight the «Gripen» is capable of carrying out maneuveres at a very low speed as is shown in this shot where it is flying with two Mi-23-«HIND» helicopters.

ADVANCED
Designed for both air-to-air and air-to-surface missions, the features of the «Gripen» make it one of the most advanced of its kind.

This aircraft, designated JAS 39(«Jakt Attack Spanning», attack and reconnaissance fighter), is being produced and delivered to operational units, thus demonstrating a continued and advanced independence in the conception and construction of weapon systems.

The project

In June 1980 an ambitious project began with the conception, design, amd materialization of a lightweight combat aircraft which incorporated the latest advances in technology; and which was capable of operating in an independent way from its eventual base camps, such as specially prepared stretches of motorway or specific streets in urban areas.

In its design stage the name «Griffin» was chosen which refers to a mythological animal.

The requirements

After analyzing various proposals from outside the country, none of which matched up to the high operational requirements. The initial needs were put together in a document which was ready on the 3rd of June 1981. After obtaining government approval on the 6th of May in 1982 a development contract began with the JAS industrial group and FMV. The Swedish defence administration covered the construction of five prototypes and 30 production units.

With the program confirmed in the Spring of 1983, the evaluation of different components began with the radar and head up display, making use of «Viggen» type aircraft in the process. The initial results were very encouraging with all the time schedules being met including the delivery of a prototype on the 26th of April 1987, which then carried out its first flight on the 19th of December 1988. However, problems with the flight management system were detected, causing two accidents one of which meant the destruction of the prototype on the 2nd of February 1989, slowing down the trials.

Validation

External support was negotiated, principally from the United States, to solve the problems derived from inadequate software and others arising from the fuel system; the starting mechanism and avionics refrigera-

tion. The fitting out of the aircraft continued with, in 1989, the inclusion of a two seater version. The remaining four prototypes flew between May 1990 and October 1991.

Using two structures for the verification of fatigue trials, in 1993 a 16,000 hours research program was created to test its durability and lifespan. A short time before, on the 3rd of June 1992 to be exact, an order for 110 units of the second batch was approved which included improved software, a new flight control system, provision for the TARAS communication equipment, optimized processors and different camouflage.

Production

With the gradual delivery of the first production aircraft, with the first flight on the 10th of September 1992. The process of creating operational units began with the first 30 units being received at the end of 1996. The first twin-seater was also delivered earlier that same year. In June 1997 the Swedish government announced the purchase of 64 new JAS 39s from the third batch. These incorporated various updates including an improved engine, they were declared operational in September 1997. After three weeks of intensive exercises the F7 wing squadron was stationed at Satenas base.

If the number of units ordered doesn't increase and present production levels stay the same, 204 «Gripen» will be delivered to

12 operational squadrons before the year 2007; with the next squadron expected to have this aircraft being the Angelholm F10 wing. However, if we take into consideration earlier developments, it is possible that an additional batch will be incorporated into this number making it unnecessary to keep the «Viggen» in active service, which will improve the logistics chain and add mission capability.

A multi-purpose airplane

Conceived with specific mission criteria,

the aim being as much self-sufficiency as possible. The JAS offers many good qualities in the evolving world of aerial combat and with a notable capability as a medium range interceptor. It can be employed against surface vessels at sea and is capable of carrying out precision attacks in the support of its own ground troops as well as destroying important enemy targets.

Multinational

Although there has been the desire to maintain that the development of this airplane and the taking on of such an ambitious project is the fruit of capable Swedish industry, and the willpower of its politicians. The final cost would make such a decision unthinkable in the majority of European countries where such manufac-

turing is done together to reduce costs. The truth, not diminishing the efforts made by its own companies, is that they have had to turn to companies from the United States ,The United Kingdom, Germany and France who have supplied important components such as the propulsion system, flight control computer, flaps control, secondary power system, electrical generator, HOTAS control system, head up display, hydraulic system and cannon.

This was demonstrated half way through 1995,with the important agreement between Saab and British Aerospace, that a multinational collaboration reduces risks and avoids long and costly development. British Aerospace had participated in the design and manufacture of the wings from the beginning of the program, to produce a «Gripen» version for export to international markets. As a result they have presented various configurations, including different engines, to avoid possible United States sanctions to countries such as Chile, Brazil,

EXPORTATION

Being presented in recent international aviation show rooms, the Saab-British Aerospace JAS-39 «Gripen» has the possibility of getting export contracts from South America as well as the Middle East.

South Africa, Hungary, Poland, The United Arab Emirates and The Czech Republic. These could be fruitful with contracts consolidating the present production capacity.

Some advanced characteristics

Defined as the first fighter of the fourth generation put into service, this model presents straightforward operational qualities and simplified maintenance, allowing staff to carry out in 10 minutes all the operations necessary to allow a new mission to proceed. This involving the loading of new weapons, checking oil levels, the detection of possible system breakdowns, and checking of the main external components.

The PS-05/A multi-mode Doppler Radar is the fruit of collaboration between Ericsson Radio and the British company Ferranti, it relys on a carbon fiber arial which allow it to detect targets during ground, air and sea search missions, while following the terrain and avoiding obstacles it also controls weaponry such as cannons

TECHNICAL CHARACTERISTICS

COST:	Approx. 50 million dollars inc. development	External fuel	2.000 kg
DIMENSIONS:		**PROPULSION:**	A RM12 WITH 8,165 KG OF THRUST
Length	14.1 m	**PERFORMANCE:**	
Height	4.5 m	Ceiling service height	15,000 m
Wingspan	8.4 m	Low altitude speed	Mach 1.08
WEIGHTS:		Runway length	800 m
Empty	6,622 kg	Combat range	800 km
Maximum	13,000 kg	Extended range	3,000 km
Max. external load	3-4 tonnes	Design load factor	+ 9 g
Internal fuel	2,268 kg		

and missiles. Associated with this, and displayed on the three multi-functional CRT screens, is one for a FLIR infra-red sensor or laser, which facilitate reaching long range targets quicker.

A total of 40 processors have the task of monitoring the different flight and system parameters, including a triple digital flight system from Lear Astronics, HOTAS controls system, optical diffraction Head Up Display (HUD), a conventional joystick control, with artificial touch designed by the British Page Engineering. The ejector seat is a Martin Baker S10LS.

Mono-engine

Based on the United States General Electric F404, the Swedish companies Volvo Air and Saab have developed an optimized version designated RM12, with a length of 404 centimeters and a weight of 1,055 kg. Thanks to the greater volume of air and a higher operating temperature they have managed to increase the performance to 8,615 kg of thrust, being able to reach Mach 1.08 without the need to resort to re-heat.

With simple and economical maintenan-

ARMED

All kinds of missiles, bombs and rockets can be installed in the «Gripen» enabling it to execute the most complex of combat missions.

WEAPONRY	
MISSION	COMPONENT
Air-to-Air	Short range «Sidewinder» infrared missiles deignated 'L' or RB 74 forthe Swedish designation.
	Soon there will be the Iris
	T medium range AIM-120
	«AMRAAM» guided missile
	In the near future is the medium range «Meteor» guided missile.
Air-to-surface	Conventional and laser guided bombs.
	Rockets
	Submunitions magazine
	AGM-65 or RB75 «Maverick» guided missiles
Anti-ship attack	Saab RB15F independent missiles
Various	Mauser BK27 de 27 mm
	cannon incorporated in the fuselage

COCKPIT

The cockpit has advanced digital displays and rationally configured equipment, with all functions optimized for the pilot's use.

ce, the new engine includes an electrical and mechanical fuel system with a consumption of 4.2 kgs of fuel per second when producting maximum power. It includes a larger diameter fan which is 15% lighter than the original the front end of the engine has also been made more robust as a protection measure against a bird strike.

Looking ahead to the future. They have begun making contacts with the German company Dasa and with the United States Boeing/Rockwell International consortium to input the necessary technology which would allow the development of a RB12 engine version. This has vectorized thrust TVC (Thrust Vector Control), initially destined for the export market.

esigned as a lightweight and economical fighter, the development of a version for naval use demonstrated its qualities and possibilities as a multi-purpose airplane. During more than three million hours of flight it has made new records in safety, operational readiness, maintainability, and mission capability. This has created

OUTSTANDING QUALITIES

Its conception came about half-way through the 1970's, and with its flight qualities, associated systems capability, robustness, reliability as demonstrated to its operators, and its weaponry possibilities, the F-18 is an aircraft which few others can match.

TOTAL PRECISION

Involved in training activities or employed in operational tasks the «Hornet» demonstrates day to day its capability to carry out all kinds of missions. Here it is dropping free-fall bombs in the competition "Low Country Bombing Derby".

notable sales success and continuous production which will be maintained until the end of the first decade of the 21st century.

Development

In the spring of 1974 the United States Navy made its VFAX program requirements known, for it to be equipped with a lightweight

multi-mission low-cost fighter. It was obligated by a Congress decision to consider the prototypes YF-16 & YF-17 by General Dynamics and Northrop respectively, which were being evaluated by the Air Force.

While the comparative studies were being carried out, McDonnel Douglas proposed an optimized version, designated the F-17, in which Northrop was an associate partner. It was this which was chosen to be developed as a naval model, given the identification NACF (Naval Air Combat Fighter). The fighter version was renamed as the F-18 and the attack version as the A-18, but the conclusion was reached that the intermediate version F/A -18 could carry out both roles without any problems. It was therefore given the generic name F-18, and received the name Hornet.

Flight of the prototype

Specific development work began on the 22nd of January 1976, and on the 18th of November 1978 the first of eleven YF-18 prototypes flew. Two of these were twin-seaters with complete combat capability, but with 6% less fuel capacity in the internal tanks.

The first F-18A was delivered to the US Navy in May 1980. After evaluation trials on aircraft carriers, the first squadron was operational two years later. Included with these were the twin-seater type B versions, and with these «Black Knights» the Marine Corps reached full combat capacity. Navy pilots of the VFA-113 «Stinger» squa-

dron began to receive theirs on the 26th of March 1983. In 1985 part of the 14th Air Wing was incorporated aboard the aircraft carrier USS «Constellation» CV-64.

Advanced Versions

Between 1986 and 1987 the F-18C & D versions were produced, a combat single-seater and twin-seater respectively, the latter for a combination of uses such as combat or training. The «Night Attack» version was ready on the 6th of May 1988, it is compatable with the C/D type, including improvements to the avionics to allow precision attacks in any weather conditions during the day or night.

This version was the standard with few modifications until 1991, when a proposal for a bigger, more capable version was presented. This received the designation F-18E/F «Super Hornet». Work began in June 1992, and the prototype for this new version flew on the 29th of November

INCREASED POTENTIAL

The US Navy has the intemtion of purchasing between six and eight hundred F-18E/F <<Super Hornet>> aircraft, with which it will replace the older versions, increasing its operational capability in both air combat and precision attack missions, depending on what has been assigned to it.

OPERATING IN SPAIN

We can appreciate the lines of the Spanish F-18 twin seater which is shown flying above Zaragoza shortly after carrying out a training mission at the firing range at Bardena Reales.

MULTIPURPOSE COMBAT AIRCRAFT

The multipurpose possibilities of the «Hornet» for all kinds of combat missions, operating from both aircraft carriers and ground bases, have been the reason for its sales success with a large number of units purchased or with countries waiting to do so.

1995, carrying out the first aircraft operations with the aircraft carrier USS «John C. Stennis» CVN-74 on the 18th of January 1997. Production of these units began, determined by the budget, this same year.

Some outstanding characteristics

Manufactured by McDonnel Douglas, the F-18 is capable of playing the role of aerial defence fighter as well as a precision attack airplane, and its success lies in its multipurpose nature and operational capability.

The cockpit

The single and combat/training twin-seater versions both incorporate a cockpit which stands out above other lightweight fighters in active service at this moment, due to a rational and ergonomic design adapted to the requirements.

Three large CRT digital screens are noteworthy for presenting a combination of data in respect to radar, weapon systems, flight parameters and operation possibilities. At the same time there is a HUD system reflecting the platform's data so that the pilot doesn't have to stop monitoring

outside the aircraft. The pilot is sits on a Martin-Baken SJU-5/6 ejector seat, and is kept comfortable thanks to air conditioning and complete pressurization.

Propulsion plant

It incorporates two powerful General Electric double flow jet engines, with little interconnection. They contain some excellent general features such as, for example, the ability to engage maximum re-heat in only 3 or 4 seconds, good acceleration capability, and increased survival prospects in the case of engine failure.

The first versions, the F404-GE-400 model, with re-heat produces 7,258 kg of thrust. The most recent versions have the F-404-GE-402 EPE (Enhanced Performance Engine) which produces 7,983 kg of thrust, while the «Super Hornet», which has been evaluated with the F-414-GE-400, produces 9,979 kg of thrust. To guarantee its operation for the longest time possible existing aircraft incorporate internal fuel tanks with a capacity of 6,061 liters, together with three sub-wing fixing points to locate auxiliary tanks with a capacity of 1,250 or 1,810 liters. The F version has been designed to hold nearly two thousand liters of additional fuel.

Capability

It has a lot of potential for both aerial combat and many types of precision attack missions based on the acceleration capability supplied by the engines and its good combat qualities in various air-to-air and air-to-surface configurations. This is also taking into account the possibilities offered by its Hughes AN/APG-65 or 73 multi-mode radar, which detects targets located nearly a hundred kilometers away.

COMBAT MISSIONS

LOCATION	YEAR	PARTICIPATION	MISSIONS
• Libya/USA crisis	1986	Aircraft from from VFA-131, 132,314 & 323 squadrons.	-Aerial defence -Air-to-surface Guided weapon attacks of patrol boats & corvettes. -Interception of MIG 23 & 25, Mirage F-1 & Sukhoi aircraft.
• Kuwait invasion by Iraq	1990-91	F-18 aircraft of the Marine Corps, the Navy and Canada (Three F-18s were lost in combat).	Attacking ground & air defences -Shot down an Iraqi MIG-23 with AIM-7M "Sparrow" missiles from a F-18. -Sank various patrol boats by cannon fire or "Hornet" bombs. -Shot down two MIG-21s with AIM-9L missiles.
• Peace process in the former Yugoslavia	1994-95	Eight F-18A+ of the Spanish & United States Air Forces.	Aerial support operation for ground troops. -Use of: >BR-250 free fall bombs >GBV-16 laser guided bombs >AGM-656 "Maverik" missiles >AGM-88 "Harm" anti-radar missiles >Air to air missiles: AIM-9LI "Sidewinder" & AIM-7F "Sparrow"

In air-to-air missions the radar is able to locate aerial targets, and offers the pilot information as to which poses the greater threat and manages medium-range guided missile systems. Meanwhile, in air-to-ground missions, it supplies an accurate representation of the terrain over which the aircraft is flying and the targets which have to be hit and, in addition, allowing very low altitude tactical flying.

In addition the aircraft is also equipped with the powerful AN/AYK-14 digital computer, wich is the computer that identifys the threat. This made up of a display screen informing the pilot of the zone that the signals are coming from, guidance and tracking radars, and different decoy flare launchers. Using Tracor AN/ALE-40 for Spanish units, or Goodyear AN/ALE-39/47 for United States units; communication equipment in UHF, HF, DF; the Tacan Collins AN/ARN-118; the inertial navigator etc, electronic war equipment can be installed in pods below the fuselage if the mission demands it. These consist of laser designators, cameras for tracking and guidance, or tactical reconnaissance equipment.

The robust under carriage designed for use on aircraft carriers allows it to operate on unprepared runways. The arrester hook allows

NAVAL DEVELOPMENT

The «Hornet» was created as a naval airplane for which it incorporated basic characteristics for its use on aircraft carriers: a robust main undercarriage to support landings, the hook which allows it to grip the arrest cable and the two jet engines which guarantee maximum survival.

NAVAL FIGHTER BOMBER

As a naval attack machine the F-18 can launch its AGM-84 «Harpoon» anti-ship missiles against naval units up to a radius of 100 kilometers or employ the SLAM (Standoff Land Attack Missile) version to attack with precision every kind of surface target located within similar distances.

Weaponry

Depending on the version, the nine to eleven external fixing points allow the transportation of between 7 to 8 tons of arms. These include AIM-9 <<Sidewinder>> short-range air-to-air missiles; AIM-7 <<Sparrow>> or AIM-120 AMRAAM medium-range missiles, it is being able to carry up to six of the former and four of the latter. This is complemented by a multi-barrel Vican M61A1 cannon made up of six 20mm rotating barrels, fed by a loader of 570 rounds and with an continuous rate of fire of up to 4,000 rounds per minute.

Missions against surface targets allow the use of a wide range of arms, which among others include, the free fall bombs Mk82, Mk83 and Mk84; other bombs such as the GBU10 & 12, CBU-59 cluster bombs, roc-

it to catch the arrester cables when it lands on the deph of an aircraft carrier, the hidden nozzle located in the upper front part allows it to refuel in flight and other equipment consists of BITE (Built In Test Equipment), a self diagnosis system which considerably reduces maintenance work and localization of component failure in particular.

ket-launchers, and various types of AGM-65 <<Maverik>> missiles which allow precision attacks on targets; anti-radar AGM-88 <<Harm>> missiles, anti-ship AGM-84 «Harpoon» missiles with a range of some 100 kilometers and its multipurpose version SLAM; B57 tactical nuclear bombs.

EFFICIENT ENGINE

The propulsion plant of the C/D versions and earlier models have been modified, and consist of two powerful General Electric jet engines F404-GE-402 EPE (Enhanced Performance Engine) with low compression, reduced consumption and virtually no visible emissions. They are installed at an angle to line up the exhaust nozzles and are capable of giving a total thrust of 14,944 kilograms and of using both JP4 & JP5 as fuel.

ROBUST LANDING CARRIAGE

Designed for use on aircraft carriers, the front landing carriage has a new wheel and is very robust; in addition the two fuselage undercarriage units incorporate a system which allows the absorption of hard impacts. These features allow the "Hornet" to also operate from superficially prepared runways.

FOLDABLE WINGS

Designed for naval use, it is possible to fold the wings which facilitating transport operations and improving its positioning in hangers or maintenance workshops.

CHAFF LAUNCHERS

Survival during combat missions is guaranteed by its agility, the capability of its electronic equipment to neutralize threats and the use of chaff launchers incorporated in the underside of the fuselage. These fire cartridges which produce an electromagnetic or infra-red signature confusing seek missiles.

TECHNICAL CHARACTERISTICS

	F-18A	F-18C	F-18E
COST IN MILLIONS OF DOLARS:	30	38	40 approx.
DIMENSIONS:			
Length	17.07 m	17.07 m	18.31 m
Height	4. 66 m	4.66 m	4.88 m
Wingspan incl. guided missile-launchers	12.31 m	12.31 m	13.68 m
Width of foldable wings	8.38 m	8.38 m	—
Wing surface area	37.16 m²	37.16 m²	46.45 m/s
Flaps surface area	2.27 m²	2.27 m²	—
WEIGHTS:			
Empty	10,455 kg	10,810 kg	13,387 kg
Maximum	25,401 kg	25,501 kg	29,937 kg
Max external load	7,711 kg	7,031 kg	8,051 kg
Internal fuel load	4.926 kg	4.926 kg	6,500 kg

External fuel load	3,053 kg	3,053 kg	3,053 kg
PROPULSION:			
Two General Electric engines	F-404-GE-400	F-404-GE-402	F-414-GE-400
Unitary power with post combustion	7,258 kg	7,983 kg	9,979 kg
PERFORMANCE:			
Ceiling service height	15,240 m	15,240 m	15,240 m
Speed at high altitude	+ Mach 1,8	+ Mach 1,8	+ Mach 1,9
Speed at low altitude	+ Mach 1	+ Mach 1	+ Mach 1,1
Runway length	427 m	427 m	380 m
Interception range	740 km	537 km	722 km
Extended range	3,326 km	3,326 km	4,000 km
Design load factor	7.5 g	7.5 g	8 g

OPTIMIZED COCKPIT

Designed to help the continual work of the pilot, it inclu-des three large cathode ray tube display screens for dif-ferent functions, A Head Up Display (HUD), a Martin Baker SJU-5/6 ejector seat, a flight control and weapons joystick and other complementary components.

INTEGRATED NOZZLE

On the front right side of the F-18 is the in flight refue-ling nozzle,automatically brought in & out, allowing it to receive fuel from tanker aircraft. Using this technique allows a significant increase in the radius of action for combat air patrol missions and those for COMMAO type actions.

ALL WEATHER CAPABILITY

Electronic equipment associated with the F-18 such as this FLIR (Forward Looking Infra Red) pod installed below the fuselage where medium range air-to-air mis-siles are normally carried, guarantees operational capa-bility in any kind of atmospheric condition, day and night.

ADVANCED RADAR

The Hughes AN/APG-65 multi-mode digital radar is capa-ble of tracking 10 aerial targets located within an 80 kilo-meters radius, presenting six of them to the pilot who can choose different air-to-air or air-to-surface modes depending on the mission which to be executed. It is a modular construction for maintenance purposes and is able to cope well with electronic counter measures.

The F-15 is considered to be the most advanced multipurpose fighter in service, boasting since entering service a record of one hundred combat victories without any aircraft lost. It caused the loss of 34 of 41 Iraqi aircraft which were shot down in combat during the Gulf war.

An advanced design

Knowledge of the Soviet Mig-25 interceptor's capabilities led the United States to program the construction of an aircraft capable of facing up to it, with studies for a new fighter with aerial superiority beginning in 1965. After evaluating the proposals of three different corporations, McDonnell Douglas was contracted to produce 18 single and 2 twin-seater aircraft for experimental trials. The first of the YF-15A single-seaters flew on the 27th of July 1972 and the first of the twin-seaters on the 7th of July the following year.

The contract

With the concept validated the first production units were contracted in accordance with the 1974 budget. The first of 572 A/B versions were received on the 14th of November 1974

and the last in 1979. This same year, on the 26th of February to be exact, the first in a series of close to 500 improved units flew, identified by the letters C/D , holding an additional 907 kg of fuel.

After coming to a commercial agreement, the Japanese company Mitsubishi was allowed to manufacture this model, and the first of two hundred F-A5J/DJs assembled in Japan were ready on the 26th of August 1981. These included radar warners and specially designed electronic war equipment. This was inferior to that of the United States, for which, from the 20th of June 1985 it was decided to apply the MSIP (Multi Staged Improvement Program), modernizing the Hughes AN/APG-63 radar to convert it to the AN/APG-70 model with greater memory

---

EXCLUSION

With the capability of carrying more than eleven tons of weaponry, the F-15E can carry out exclusion missions where it will attack ground objectives over a long distance or play an air defence role against multiple targets, day and night or in bad weather.

IMPLEMENTATION

From its origins as an interceptor with a wide radius of action the «Eagle» has been evolved up to the point of being a very advanced multipurpose fighter bomber to which few countries can get access due to government and economic restrictions (photograph below).

MISSIONS

F-15C FIGHTER BOMBER	F-15E ATTACK AIRCRAFT
- Combat air patrols (CAP)	- Aerial superiority & defence
- Aerial superiority & defence	- Nuclear attack
- Long distance interception	- Bomb & missile attacks against surface targets
- Satellite attacks (ASAT)	- Defence against: cruise missile attacks (CMD) and ballistic missile attacks (TDM). Anti-aircraft defence suppression(SEAD) and reconnaissance (being evaluated)

capacity and data processing, and installing a new Honeywell weapon control panel improving the defensive electronic war combination.

A multipurpose fighter

At the same time as the incorporation of new accessories to the aircraft in service, there emerged the need to evaluate the capability of the «Eagle», with respect to carrying out both attack missions and the gaining of aerial superiority, for which a twin-seater was modified. With satisfactory results from the trials, planners ordered the mass production of two hundred E version twin-seaters, the first of which was delivered on the 12th of April 1988 and based at Luke base in Arizona. The last was delivered during 1996.

Specializing in all weather precision attacks the «Strike Eagle», as it has been designated, operates with specific equipment which includes synthetic aperture radar, modified to give better resolution when it is working in a ground tracking mode, FLIR infra-red seeker, Martin Marieta LANTIRN attack and navigation system,

OPTIMIZATION

It's equipment, capability, and size give it multiple possibilities for deployment in both defence and attack missions in which, it should always be successful.

MULTIPURPOSE

Considered to be the most advanced fighter bomber at the moment, the F-15 is used by the United States, Israel, Saudi Arabia and Japan, countries which put a great deal of resources into maintaining armed forces with real capabilities for both deterrence and attack.

made up of the AN/AAQ-13 navigation unit and AN/AAQ-14 attack unit. This at the same time as subsequent cockpits including four display screens allowing the sharing of the workload among the two crew members, and the aircraft with a capability of carrying a payload of more than 11 tons.

Exportation of the F-15

The capability of this aircraft to carry out a dual role, as demonstrated during the Gulf War, led to the preparation of a proposal specifically aimed at export markets. Initially

receiving the designation H. Still with, some limitations in the equipment and capabilities, from 1994 it has been purchased by Israel with code F-15I, and by Saudi Arabia as the F-15S. The Japanese, however, decided to improve theirs with more advanced electronic equipment, faster and up rated processors, and with the 220E engine version which now offers greater power and substantial improvements to its performance.

To evaluate future concepts and to face up to the aggressive export policy of

Russia, a modified F-15B was prepared, coming under the STOL/MTD (Short Take Off and Landing/ Maneuvere Technology Demonstrator) program equipped with engines incorporating directional nozzles in two axes and advanced flow reversers, thanks to which it has demonstrated its capability to make ultra-short landings in spaces between 15 and 457 meters.

An advanced airplane

More than 1,200 A,B,C,D & E type units have been purchased by the United States Air Force, and those remaining in service, among front line units, the Reserve and National Air Guard , come to a total of 746. A larger number of these are needed in reserve, and are currently in AMARC storage zones at the Davis-Monthan base in Arizona. To these can be added the 90 A/B/C/D aircraft remaining in Israel from the hundred purchased, and the twenty five I aircraft optimized and in the process of being handed over. 147 were built in Japan under licence; 76 C and 72 S aircraft purchased by Saudi Arabia, 24 of which have the latest upgrades for aerial superiority missions, and 48 are prepared for surface attacks.

ATTACK

With its pay load capacity, range (due to the internal fuel tank load), and the potential of its systems to destroy any kind of target, this aircraft continues to be the standard-against which other designs are measured.

DEPLOYMENT

The USAF, Reserve & National Air Guard are often deployed to different parts of the world to participate in many tydes of exercises, demonstrating their potential to face any aggressor.

Its structure

With an aerodynamic design which allows it to reach high speed at high altitude, its Lear Astronics digital flight control enables it to carry out missions in an automatic terrain tracking mode. Structurally many of its components have been made with honey-combed panels of aluminium and graphite/epoxy fibres. For reinforcment there has been the extensive use of titanium and plastic derivatives; 60% of the E version's structure has been modified to allow for 16,000 hours of useful life at a high number of g's.

It has three undercarriage components, with one wheel for each and a pneumatic absorption system for operation on semi-

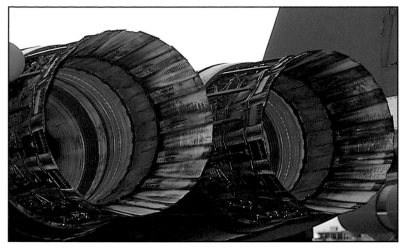

threat, this coming from a winning design and a combination of advanced systems. One of the more notable of these is the AN/APG-70 Hughes Aircraft Doppler Radar which operates in band X for the fighter version and L for the attack version, having a capability to detect and follow targets which are almost 150 kilometers away.

Its programmable signal processor detects and fixes on small flying targets at very high speeds at any altitude, and in close combat this target is hit automatically. The data from the sensors and information on the best weapons for attack it go through the McDonnell Douglas AN/AVQ-20 Head Up Display and are interrogated by the AN/APX-101 IFF Teledyne Electronics system to establish if the target

prepared runways. Two large tails, a large aileron on the upper center part of the craft, and two wings set back on the fuselage, all of which correspond to a design which is optimized for a response to current needs.

POWERFUL

The C & E version turbofans are very advanced, robust models providing agility in close aerial combat.

MODEL C TECHNICAL CHARACTERISTICS

COST:	55 million dollars		External fuel load	9,817 kg
DIMENSIONS:			**PROPULSION:**	Two F-100-PW-220 Pratt & Whitney turbofans
Length	19.43 m			with 10,770 kg of thrust each.
Height	5.63 m		**PERFORMANCE:**	
Wingspan	13.05 m		Service ceiling height	18,300 m
Surface Wing area	56.50 m²		Speed at high altitude	+Mach 2,5
			Speed at low altitude	Mach 1,21
WEIGHTS:			Runway length	274 m
Empty	12,973 kg		Interception range	1,200 km
Maximum	30,845 kg		Extended range	5,745 km
Max. external load	10,705 kg		Design load factor	9 g
Internal fuel load	6,103 kg			

Power

In this sense the two engines are located close together along the central axis , allowing the aircraft to continue to fly in the case that one engine fails. The F-100-PW-220 Pratt & Whitney jet engines have been substituted by the 229 model since 1991. This version offers 12,200 kilograms of thrust for each engine with re-heat. This gives it enough power to achieve a level of flight performance in which it acquits itself well in any combat phase. Additionally, it can take off from very short runways and climb almost vertically at a speed of 15,000 meters per minute.

Replying to threats

With more than enough power, it has an unequalled capability to face any aerial

TWIN SEATER

Multipurpose versions include a twin-seater cockpit, similar to the training unit, increasing mission possibilities with the pilot and systems operator sharing the workload.

is a friend or enemy. Surface attack data is presented on a multifunction screen and holographic display in front of the pilot, allowing the terrain to be followed accurately at low altitude, by using maps of the zone over which it is flying, which guarantes the successful use of weapons whether they are dropped or launched from the aircraft.

Weaponry

The pilots have an elevated position, sitting in zero-zero type ejector ACES II seats which can be launched at any altitude. They also enjoy excellent visibility both forwards and back. This capability allows them to execute their missions with a greater guarantees of success. The normal weapons carried for air-to-air actions include the General Electric M61A1 20mm cannon with 512 rounds, 4 AIM-9 «Sidewinder» infra-red missiles; 4 AIM-7 «Sparrow» and 8 «AMRAAM» AIM-120 radar-guided missiles.

In surface attacks the Dynamics Control Corporation AN/AWG-27 weapon control system is very useful and can be used to employ precision missiles such as the AIM-65 «Maverik», together with different bombs including the conventional Mk82 & Mk84; the Mk20 «Rockeye», the guided bombs GBU-10,12,15 & 25, the self-propelled AGM-130 for attacks at safe distances, and the nuclear B61.

ARMED

With a multi-barreled cannon incorporated in the upper part of the fuselage side and multiple fixing points below the wings and the central structure, the «Strike Eagle» can be provided with a wide range of weapon systems and associated equipment.

For self defence it relies on a Northrop Grumman AN/ALQ-135(V) automatic type electronic counter-measure system; Magnavox AN/ALQ-128 radar emissions detector; RWR Loral AN/ALR-56C equipment; Tracor AN/ALE-45 decoy flare launchers.

REQUIREMENTS

The size of the aircraft and its equipment possibilities require a large and specialized maintenance team at the landing base to guarantee its operational readiness.

The Russian response to western technical advances in aviation has not been to sit idly by. Its latest aircraft are impresive in their design capability, maneuverability and sophistication. This widespread and well established line of new products has led the Russian firm Sukhoi to design models which can compete in an aggressive market. Its products, at the moment, are noteworthy with their considerable power, and it is hoped that they will enter the market in the near future, continuing the export tradition begun with the Su15, Su-17, Su-20 and Su-22 which have been sold to countries such as Afghanistan, Czechoslovakia, Algeria, Egypt, Poland, Syria, Yemen and Vietnam.

The Sukhoi's progress

Earlier aircraft became well-established leading the firm's designers to the development of a new attack aircraft model. Known at the beginning as the Su-19 «Fencer A», later in 1976, when the production of operational units began, this became the Su-24 Fencer B , with more than 900 units constructed in the Kom-somolsk factories. It has an outstanding

EXPORT

With the objective of obtaining the best external sales success possible, the Su-30K twin-seater has been built, existing in different multipurpose versions and exported to countries such as India and Indonesia, with a number of other countries interested in purchasin it.

FLANKER

Optimized for air-to-air missions the Su-27 was the Soviet reply to western designs which entered service in the 1980's, and with its advanced configuration it demonstrates an agility which surpasses other fighter aircraft.

capacity for neutralizing ground positions when flying at low altitude, with a flight profile optimized by varying the angle of the wings. Different versions have been developed, M with terrain tracking radar, MR with reconnaissance and electronic war equipment and MP with electronic disruption equipment, all of which were in service during the 1980's.

Lightweight attacker

Known for its initial role in the Afghanistan war, during which 23 were shot down, the Su-25 «Frogfoot» is a small airplane specializing in close support work and in the attack of troops on the battlefield. Operational since 1984 and exported to Afghanistan, Iraq, lovakia, Hungary and Bulgaria, it has served as the base for the UB operational conversion and weapons training units; the UGT for naval deployment; the BM equipped with aerial targets for fighter pilot training; and the UT which was presented in

have ended up in Russian combat squadrons and have been exported to China in various batches totalling some eighty aircraft. It is notable for its aerodyna-

1989 as the Su-28.

Developed from this last aircraft, the Su-25 was introduced in 1991, optimized for anti-tank missions thanks to its laser-guided missiles and 30mm double cannon. This along with the new Su-39 lightweight twin-engined attack aircraft, which with five fixing points for weapons and equipment on each of its wings and one on the underside of the fuselage, can carry 4.36 tons of weaponry which can be launched during day and night attacks due to the navigation and weapon firing systems incorporated.

INTERCEPTOR
The design and components making up the construction of the Su-30K fighter give it some very good features for carrying out interception tasks it is capable of launching a large number of advanced weapons.

Features of the interceptor

Initially known as the «Ram-J», after being detected by United States spy satellites, the Su-27 Flanker is a real indicator of Russia's design capability in high performance interceptors. After flying in 1981, more than two hundred units of this model

OPERATION
After 15 years in service with the Russian Air Force, a period of time in which it has demonstrated its operational possibilities, the design of the Su-27 has been optimized to serve as the base for a new generation of fighters such as Su-30, Su-35, Su-37.

mic shape and powerful engines which give it an agility which is superior to other occidental designs. At the same time it has a high maximum velocity, a large capacity to incorporate all kinds of advanced air-to-air missiles and a combat mission radius put at around 1,500 kilometers, all of which are excellent features for this long-range, all-weather interceptor.

Developed from the previous aircraft is the outstanding Su-30K fighter which is a twin-seater aircraft capable of operating in any weather conditions thanks to a Doppler type radar, which has the capability of detecting 10 targets in a 100km radius and engaging two of them it also has an optics and infra-red system for firing control; a maximum weight of 30,450 kg, of which 8,000 kg is the pay load and a maximum range of 3,000 km without refueling. In April 1997 the first 8 Su-30M's arrived in India, a multi-purpose version of the K model, with additional deliveries continuing up to the year 2001 with 32 additional Mk1 units. These include two AL-31FU jets with directional thrust control, in flight refueling capability, twelve positions for the loading of weapons and a maximum weight of 38 tons. Indonesia recently ordered 12 Su-30MK units.

The naval fighter

Designed along the lines of earlier models, the long range Su-32FN naval attack plane is a twin-seater with an armored cockpit arranged so that the pilot and wea-

pons operator sit side-by-side. The engines are significantly apart from each other to improve aerodynamics. This naval fighter has specific equipment and systems dedicated to it, such as a strengthened front undercarriage with two wheels allowing it to operate from semi-prepared runways. The cockpit incorporates a combination of analogue displays for flight parameters and four large digital display screens for tracking and attacking.

Identified earlier as the Su-271B, it was exhibited at Bourget in 1995 and 1997, and is designated to attack naval targets such as hostile surface ships and submarines. Tasks for which it has an artificial intelligence system supporting the crew members in critical situations. There is a specialized search radar and sonar buoy launcher with a capacity of 72 units, magnetic anomalies detector, infra-red equipment and laser rangefinder, complemented with a wide range of weapons with which it can attack naval and aerial targets in a 250 km radius.

Looking to the future

The Russian Air Force is still deciding if it should incorporate the Su-35 into its aerial arsenal. This is an advanced version developed from the «Flanker» with directional thrust and a multipurpose capability and whose inclusion is still not clear due to the government's financial problems. While the air force has been trying to make a decision, the new experimental Su-37 design has been flying since 1996, propelled by two AL-37FU Satum/Lyulka jet engines incorporating asymmetric nozzles which together produce 28,500kg of thrust. It has great agility, incorporating an electronic control system for all its moveable components, including the nozzles, as a result of the speed and altitude of the aircraft and with the N011M radar it can instantaneously look for aerial and surface tarjets. Its basic characteristics are a length of 22.2 meters, weight of 25.7 tons and it carries the most advanced missiles among which

IMPRESSIVE
Large, heavy, robust, powerful and capable are some of the characteristics which define land-based naval attack plane Su-32FN being developed by the Russian Air Force and which could pose a serious threat for occidental surface units.

OUTSTANDING
The capability of new designs coming from the Sukhoi laboratory has borne fruit with the display of a wide and varied range of models characterized by outstanding features among which can be found the Su-32FN designed as a long distance attack aircraft, replacing the Su-24 «Fencer».

are the air-to-air R-37 & KS-172, air-to-surface X-15P, and the stealth X-65S.

The existence of a new lightweight fighter became known as the result of the mock-up exhibited at the Paris Air Show in July 1997, a model which was similar to, but smaller than, the Su-35. The configuration includes canards, a twin tail and a centrally positioned Saturn AL-31F engine. It is equipped with a Sokol Falcon firing control radar with a maximum range of 180 km which will allow it to follow 4 of 24 targets it has detected. This aircraft could constitute the Russian response to the requirements of the 21st century with respect to agility, combat potential and performance.

Although it has to be developed for its qualities to be truly evaluated, some of the latest advances of this company are already known, including the fifth generation S-32/S-37, which in September 1997 first flew at the Zhukovsky Evaluation center where the noteworthy features were the inverted arrow wings, canards, and D-30F6 jet engines with vectorized thrust.

TAILS

Two large tails give it the stability necessary to execute low altitude flight above the sea, at the same time housing some secondary equipment.

PROPULSION

The two AL-31F jet engines which drive the Su-32FN produce a maximum of 25,000 kilograms of thrust, with which they can give it a maximum speed of 1.8 Mach.

RADAR HOUSING

The large and elongated protuberance located between both engines can serve to improve general stability or for housing electronic mission support equipment, including the radar.

ROBUST LANDING CARRIAGE

To satisfy the requirements of a long range naval attack airplane, it has been necessary to construct a very large and heavyweight aircraft which needs a robust main under carrige is retracted into the area where the wings and fuselage meet.

Su-32 FN TECHNICAL CHARACTERISTICS

COST:	Approx. 50 million dollars		PROPULSION:	TWO AL-31F JET ENGINES WHICH PRODUCE A UNIT THRUST OF 12,500 KG WITH RE-HEAT AND 7,500 KG WITHOUT.
DIMENSIONS:				
Length	23.3 m		**PERFORMANCE:**	
Height	6.5 m		Ceiling service height	18,000 m
Wingspan	14.7 m		Speed at high altitude	Mach 1.8
Wing surface area	62 m2	62 m²	Speed at low altitude	Mach 1.14
WEIGHTS:			Extended range	4,000 km
Maximum	44,360 kg		Design load factor	9 g's
Maximum external load	8,000 kg			

TWIN SEATER

With a duck-billed shape, the armored twin-seater cockpit houses the pilot and systems operator who together carry out the tasks entrusted to them with the support of display screens and control components, somewhat old fashioned compared with western standards but effectiv.

FUSELAGE

In the area to the rear of the cockpit is the lower entrance which gives the pilots access; the cannon which is incorporated in the fuselage; two large air intakes which feed the engines.

CANARDS

Behind and below the cockpit are two large canard fins which optimize flight at high and low altitude for this aircraft thanks to its movement which is controlled by the flight system.

Despite the fact that France was at one point in negotiations to develop a European fighter bomber along with other countries, the project designated ACE (Avion du Combat Europeen). But the pressure from its powerful defence industry , the self-sufficiency of the government in Paris and the need to have a leading export component to encourage the development of other sectors; brought about the decision to undertake a purely national project consisting of both a tactical twin-seater attack aircraft, and a single-seater interceptor with multipurpose capabilities.

The decision

While it was collaborating on the design concepts of the ACE, the Dassault company was continuing the development work on a new fighter bomber which could be its trump card for export. The first Rafale A

ON BOARD
In accordance with the requirements of the National French Navy, a specific model has been developed to operate on French aircraft carriers including the nuclear Charles de Gaulle, which is the destination for a squadron of Rafale M's which will constitute a multi-purpose component.

NAVAL VERSION
After evaluating the F-18 «Hornet» as an option, the French Navy decided to go for the naval version of the Rafale to make up the defensive-offensive component of its aircraft carriers. This was a process which required substantial changes to the components and equipment to cope with hard take-offs and landings and a hostile environment.

prototype flew on the 4th of July 1986, for which it had though it had to use general electric F404 engines, because the French engines would not being ready until February 1990.

A military aircraft

After the decision of the French military to incorporate the Rafale model in its air-fields, the development contract for a single seater "C" prototype was signed on the 21st of April 1988, and shortly after a naval prototype was requested, redesignated M101.

The C model flew in October 1991 and the M version on the 12th of December the same year. It completed a high number of trials which validated the earlier expectations. These included both the launchings carried out by catapult in a United States base at Patuxent River and on the aircraft carrier «Foch». In February 1993 it was equipped with the new Thomson-CSF/Dassault Electronique RBE2 electronic sweep radar (Radar a Bayalage Electronique) and the Spectra defensive system for the B model twin-seater.

Forecast

There is a market potential of 500 units, among which possible overseas orders can be found such as the existing proposal from the United Arab Emirates. The French Air Force & Navy have reduced their purchase expectations to 234 and 60 units respectively (with the first of these ordered on the 26th of March 1993). The M model aircraft

will be the first delivered with advanced equipment and avionics, ready for the nuclear aircraft carrier Charles de Gaulle, which being built at present and which is expected to be operational in the 14th fleet in 2002.

L'Armee de L'Air is not in a desperate hurry to have these aircraft, given that its current aerial capability allows it to carry out those missions entrusted to it, however it is expected that its aircraft will be delivered between 1998 and the year 2009. These will correspond to the multipurpose C version, and a training/low altitude penetration B version. This last version is foreseen as the aircraft to execute nuclear attack missions, provided with the advanced ASMP missile.

An operational aircraft

With three different versions developed from the beginning, all using the same fuselage, it is expected that this aircraft can achieve a useful life cycle of between 25 and 30 years; now that the program is being carried out following criteria with great potential and controlled development costs.

EVALUATION

The design and development of the Rafale has required the construction of different prototypes which combined different versions of single and twin-seaters, in accordance with the specific requirements of both the French Air Force and Navy.

SALES

The features of the Rafale and French sales policies box well for important sales success in those parts of the world where French military systems are already being used, although the high price for this aircraft will make its purchase difficult for countries with a modest budget.

Capabilities

With the capability of quickly changing its operational configuration, and able to operate day and night and in all weather conditions, its short and medium range missions include surface attack, aerial superiority, reconnaissance and high precision attacks using both conventional and nuclear weapons. For this the RBE2 radar is essential, having the capability to lock onto eight targets at the same time.

To carry out attacks the aircraft has an internal Giat DEFA 30mm cannon which operates at the rate of 2,500 rounds per minute, and it can hold more than nine tons of weapons on its 14 fixing points below the wings and fuselage (13 on the M model), these being made up of conventional and

guided bombs, submunitions housings, APA-CHE guided weapons etc. In the M version up to eight medium-range MICA missiles can be carried supplied with infra-red or active laser guidance. For reconnaissance work it is provided with a pod equipped with electronic sensors and cameras, while precision attacks are executed with AS-30L guided missiles using laser designators with the Altis and supported by a FLIR system.

Integration of capabilities

The use of advanced technologies has meant the integration of different capabilities, constituting a truly multi-purpose fighter, small in size, which will replace more than six different types of specialist aircraft in France in the future. A system of processors have been integrated which facilitate the work of the pilot, and manage the greater part of the systems with the joystick (HOTAS concept, Hands On Throttle And Stick). It has been supplied with an integrated logistic support system (ILS), enjoys very efficient aerodynamics, incorporates various refinements to significantly reduce its radar signature and has equipment completely co-ordinated for self-protection, communication and management of weapons.

Advanced components

More than thirty specialist companies have been supporting the work to create advanced components, with the Rafale designed to incorporate all of these systems. The mission computers co-ordinate parameters related to the flight control system, the working of the engines, tactical

MULTIPURPOSE

With its design, equipment and performance, the Rafale fighter bomber marks the beginning of a new generation of aircraft designed to give high levels of performance in both air-to-air and air-to-surface missions and at the same time this airplane is capable of taking off from aircraft carriers.

INFRA-RED

The short range infra-red Mk2 «Magic 2» missile is a self defence component which can be fired from points on the outside edge of the wings.

systems, mission planning, self protection, vital support components, navigation, and coded data links, offer the pilot all the information necessary to carry out his mission and manage the weaponry.

A high technology holographic viewfinder with a large surface area, a large central display screen and two smaller complementary screens offer the user everything necessary to carry out the operational requirements, guaranteeing perfect integration between man and aircraft, thanks to the pilot's position. The OBOGS independent oxygen generating system; the high definition displays; the SEMMB ejector seats inclined at an angle of 29 degrees, with a viewfinder incorporated in the helmet.

Therefore, its structure, with two moveable stub wings located above the inlet nozzles, have been designed with maximum capability in mind. Among the materials employed the most striking are the com-

posites, titanium SPF-DB, superplastics, aluminium SPF, and different components resulting from the application of Stealth technology.

Control

The FCS digital flight control system ensures that the aircraft is stable at all times. Safe flying is guaranteed thanks to continuous and automatic control of flight modes and associated components such as the autopilot, altimeter, guidance system,

MEDIUM RANGE

Provided with their own infra-red or radar guidance systems, the MICA are the main aerial combat and interception weapon of the French Rafale.

CAPABLE

With 14 fixing points , its capability for carrying all kinds of weapons, bombs, housings, auxiliary fuel tanks etc, allows it to execute a wide range of missions, being easily re-configured from one mission to another.

etc. This capability is linked with the power produced by its two SNECMA M88 jet engines which despite being smaller and lighter than other conventional designs, are the result of an advanced research process which allow the aircraft to carry out long range missions without restrictions , with a particularly low level of fuel consumption. It has reached a high operational level and is of a modular construction which guarantees a low maintenance cost and also offers a high thrust-to-weight ratio.

MODEL C TECHNICAL CHARACTERISTICS

COST:	45 million dollars
DIMENSIONS:	
Length	15.3 m
Height	5.3 m
Wingspan	10.8 m
Wing surface area	45.7 m²
WEIGHTS:	
Empty	10,000 kg
Maximum	24,500 kg
Maximum external load	9,500 kg
Internal fuel load	4,500 kg
External fuel load	7,500 kg

PROPULSION:	
2 double flow SNECMA M-88-2 jet engines with a combined thrust of 13,800 kg.	
PERFORMANCE:	
Ceiling service height	18,000 m
High altitude speed	Mach 1.8
Low altitude speed	+ Mach 1
Runway length	450 m
Interception range	1,852 km
Extended range	4,000 km
Design load factor	+ 9 g's

WARNER

On the upper part of the tail is the housing for the advanced Spectra electronic warning system designed by Thomson CSF comprising automatic countermeasure components.

POWERFUL

The two SNECMA M88-2 jet engines with increased power give a thrust of 13,88 kilograms which will be greater when the M88-3's are manufactured for production units.

WEAPONRY

All kinds of missiles and bombs can be positioned in the 14 fixing points to accomplish missions assigned to the aircraft, including housings for specific reconnaissance work.

LAUNCHABLE

For evaluation of the SEMMB Mk16 advanced ejector seat the front part of the fuselage has been used, moved at great speed along a track.

RANGE

With internal fuel tanks incorporated in the fuselage with a capacity of 5,235 liters, the auxiliary sub-wing tanks with 2,000 liters, the tank located under the fuselage with 1,700 liters and the in flight refueling nozzle, the aircraft has a tactical range which can be adapted as necessary.

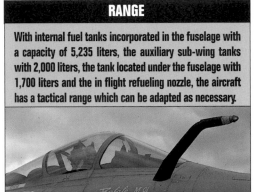

EJECTION

Accomodated in a SEMMB Mk16 ejector seat, manufactured under license from Martin-Baker, inclined at an angle of 29 degrees, the pilot enjoys excellent visibility and the ability to be safely ejected at any altitude.

DETECTORS

A Thomson-CSF/Dassault Electronique RBE 2 radar (Radar a Bayalage Elecronique, deux plans) is housed in the nose of the aircraft, with the capability of following eight targets simultaneously, complemented by infra-red and optical sensors from Thomson-TRT/SAT OSF (Optronique Secteur Frontal).

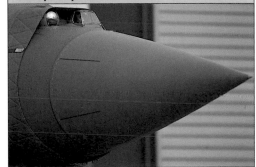

LANDING CARRIAGE

Both the front under carriage with two wheels and the double rear units are very solid and resistant, allowing it to operate from a variety of runways including the small decks of aircraft carriers.

ADVANCED

The shape of the fuselage and in particular the two air intakes have been optimized to reduce as much as possible the radar signature, making it difficult to locate. In addition there is multiple on board equipment to improve its self defence capability against all kinds of threats.

Kept secret for several years, the attacks carried out by United States aircraft against ground objectives during the operation Just Cause with the occupation of Panama on the 19th of December 1989, or in the first phases of Operation Desert Storm in January 1991 made the public aware of the general capabilities of such aircraft, in being able to avoid detection by anti-aircraft tracking and guidance radar.

The aircraft's conception

The special development division worked from 1975 on the development of certain types of shapes which changed the direction of reflected radar waves, together with the materials necessary for absorbing these waves and neutralizing the action of radar detectors, flying at night and with adequate screening of the jet engine exhausts it is very difficult to locate and intercept this aircraft.

Validation of the «Have Blue»

Using a scale model inside an wind tunnel to evaluate the design performance. Together with a full size model to measure the real result obtained, it turned out to be a design which supplied a one thousandth of the echo of earlier models. The

---

ADVANCED

Optimized to carry out specific requirements, the F-22 is now beginning a series of evaluation trials which will conclude with mass production and entry in to service in the first few years of the 21st century.

«BLACK JET»

This was the first nick name given to this small Stealth bomber which has a design and equipment optimized for carrying out extended flights up to attack zones without being detected by adversaries' radars, operating nearly always at night to avoid visual detection (photograph to the right).

---

positive results encouraged the construction of two Have Blue prototypes, the first of which flew for the first time in December 1977.

After the trials five units were tentatively ordered which were confirmed when the first unit flew from the secret installation in Tonopah in the Nevada desert on the 18th of June 1981. 59 production units followed as a result of the budgets from 1980 to 1988, which were targeted for the 4450th Tactical Group, where the preparation activities of the crew were begun along with the validation of operational procedures.

Stealth capability

Popularly known as the Stealth, the existence of the F-117A Black Jet (the name it was initially baptized with) was systematically denied by the US Air Force until the 10th of November 1988 when the first photograph was published and its

DETAILS

This front shot of the «Night Hawk» reveals some details such as the probes which capture external data, the air intakes covered by a fine grill and the infra-red tracking turret located in front of the cockpit (photograph to the right).

capabilities began to light. The last unit was received on the 12th of July 1990. In tandem to the introduction of the earlier mentioned model, created for concrete missions, design and material advances resulting from the F-117A Night Hawk's development began being introduced to other industrial designs. Always with the idea of reducing the radar signature, the results were applied to, among others, the F-18E/F Fighter Bomber; the F-22 Raptor Fighter; the A-12 Attack Aircraft and its successor the JSF (Joint Strike Fighter); the RAH-66 Commanche Helicopter and the B-2 Spirit Strategic Bomber.

The F-117A «Night Hawk»

At the moment 53 F-117A aircraft are on active duty, distributed among the 7th, 8th & 9th squadrons of the 49th Fighter Wing at Holloman base in New Mexico.

Advanced characteristics

The shapes coming out of the Lockheed Martin Skun Works, break with the ideas of aerodynamic lines from the past, and are covered with RAM materials which absorb radar waves. With these a model has been put together with a radar cross sectional area estimated at 0.01 m2. Its characteristics are: wings with a very sharp dart angle; a twin tail with the same mounting air intakes incorporated in the fuselage covered with a fine grill; flattened engine exhaust areas with heat-reflecting ceramic tiles very similar to develop-

> **EXHAUST**
> With the aim of reducing to a minimum the infra-red signature, the F-117 has been supplied with very flat exhaust nozzles made up of a configuration of small square ceramic tiles which dissipate the heat transmitted to the exterior.

ments from NASA's Space Shuttle program. A cockpit canopy whichunlike most other aircraft is not rounded and incorporating transparent panels covered with a gold film to dissipate heat.

With this shape it would be difficult to maintain stable flight, this has meant it had to incorporate a GEC Astronics quadruple type advanced digital control system, which keeps it stable at all times.

The cockpit

Sitting in an ACESII ejecter seat the aircraft pilot has a technologically advanced cockpit similar to the F-16, which some sources say it is derived from. Multi-function displays with monochrome screens, Head Up Displays (HUD) supply the pilot with basic flight data and information

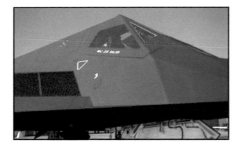

> **COCKPIT**
> With a design quite similar to that of the F-16, the single seater F-117 has been developed so that the pilot can carry out his work in an optimized way, at the same time as the aircraft's external shape reduces to a minimum the reflection of echoes back to detection radars (photograph to the left).

> **SURPRISE**
> Although the existence of an aircraft with such advanced characteristics was known inside the Defence sector, the presentation of the F-117 to the public caused surprise due to its design and features.

associated with infra-red system, coded communication equipment, a Honeywell radar altimeter and main actuator controls allow a stabile fight in any kind of weather conditions, although lacking radar.

This type of equipment is being put into practice this decade with a new and more accurate control system, color display components, new IBM processors, improved software to increase its combat capability, digital display for position, satellite positioner and a new IRADS sensor are in the process of being acquired.

Weapon guidance

Weapon guidance is carried out thanks to a stabilized Texas Instruments FLIR/DLIR including a laser designator which it is hoped will be replaced by the new IRADS. Both guide launchable weaponry which it carries inside the bomb bay and which usually consists of two 907 kg laser guided bombs of the type BLU-109B or GBU-10/27. With the size of the hold it could include the Maverik AGM-65 or Harm AGM-88 missiles or a free-fall nuclear weapon. Some sources have proposed the installation of Sidewinder air-to-air missiles in the weapon hold to give the aircraft a self-defence capability.

LANDING CARRIAGE

Consisting of a three piece carriage very similar to the F-16, the front and rear wheels are retracted forward and covered by doors to reduce the F-117's radar signature.

PROPULSION

Fed by two large air intakes designed to reduce its radar signature, the two Pratt & Whitney F119-0W-100 turbines are capable of taking the F-22 to a speed of Mach 1.7 which allows it to reach a super cruising speed without having to make use of post combustion.

Details of the F117A «Night Hawk»

It is small enough to be transported inside the fuselage of the Galaxy aircraft which gives it a strategic capacity. It has a robust three piece undercarriage designed by Menasco, with the front and rear landing carriages pulled forward and up; the fuselage is almost completely constructed out of aluminium, with titanium inserts in the engine areas and with a polymer based coating incorporating magnetic particles. These are some of the differentiating details of this aircraft.

Propelled by two General Electric F404-GE-FID2 jet engines without post combustion, derived from the F-18, and with a unit thrust of 4,900 kg, it can maintain a cruising speed of 0.9 Mach. The earlier models were fed by a fuel tank incorporated in the upper part of the fuselage, in an area

TECHNICAL CHARACTERISTICS

	F-117A	F-22		External fuel load	No	No
COST:	42,6 million dolars	90 million dolars		**PROPULSION:**	Two General Electric	Two Pratt & Whitney
DIMENSIONS:					F404-GE-F1D2	F119-PW-100
Length	20.08 m	18.92 m			jet engines	jet engines
Height	3.78 m	5.00 m			without re-heat	with re-heat
Wingspan	13.20 m	13.56 m		**PERFORMANCE:**		
Wing surface area	105.9 m²	78 m²		Ceiling service height	—	15,240 m
Flaps surface area	—	5.10 m²		Speed at high altitude	+ Mach 1	Mach 1.7
WEIGHTS:				Speed at low altitude	Mach 0.9	+ Mach 1
Empty	13,608 kg	14,365 kg		Landing speed	227 km/h	—
Maximum	23,813 kg	27,216 kg		Combat range	1,112 km	—
Maximum load	2,268 kg	2,268 kg		Extended range	2,268 km	—
Internal fuel load	—	14,000 l		Design load factor	+6 g	+ 9 g
		(estimated)				

set back from the engines, thanks to which it can cover a distance of 2,268 kilometers. This is increased with the use of in flight refueling.

The F-22 «Raptor»

Initially created to complement and then substitute the existing F-15 «Eagle», the choice of a new fighter with aerial superiority and undetectable characteristics was the challenge facing the YF-22 and YF-23 designs, the first of which, the pro-posal by Lockheed Martin Aeronautical System, was chosen.

Incidents

The initial requirements were identified in November 1981 by the USAF and the first Lockheed prototype Model 1132 was chosen in October 1986 and carried out its first flight, as the YF-22, on the 29th of September 1990. After a very complicated development process badly designed components were discovered.

PRODUCTION

The first production unit of the F-22 «Raptor» carried out its first flight on the 7th of September 1997. It is expected that trials will continue with the earlier prototypes and that the aircraft will go into service when the US Air Force gives a definite order, thus making clear the future needs.

There were failures in auxiliary power units detected, fuel losses, and inadequate software was identified. The General Accounting Office (GAO) also questioned some aspects associated with the cost-efficiency ratio. Finally, the first definitive F-22A evaluation unit, no. 4001, was delivered on the 9th of April at the Georgia factory and flew for the first time, after several delays, on the 7th of September that same year. Flown by the chief test pilot Paul Metz. After 50 test flights, the first of the 4002 units flew in 1998.

Entering service

With the Engineering and Manufacturing Development (EDM) process under way, including being taken to Edwards Air Base in a Galaxy aircraft to check parameters and performance, the discussion about the number of aircraft and when

OUTSTANDING

With a design which stands out for its angular shape which was designed to diminish the radar signature detected by its adversaries, the F-22 excels in its air-to-air combat capability and its operational survival possibilities. The power of its engines give it a high speed without using post combustion.

PRODUCTION

Shortly before carrying out its first flight on the 7th of September 1997, the first F-22 <<Raptor>> production unit became known which was different in some aspects, including performance, to the prototypes used in the initial evaluations.

they should enter service began. While the Air Force pressed for 1999's budget to include the beginning of mass production, with the number of aircraft finally to be 438, other governmental bodies also stressed its necessity, but reduced the amount to 339, significantly increasing the program's development costs.

As a result, different modifications were studied to reduce these costs, limiting its possibilities and capabilities. The elimination of the following were considered: the extendible missile launcher; the capability for carrying new Sidewinder AIM-9X missiles and JDAM (Joint Direct Attack Munition), the communication coder to transfer information between airplanes and to replace the planned radar, up to now classified and designated NBILST, for one developed from an earlier design such as the AN/APG-77. Halfway through 1997 the results of studies relating to an E version twin seater attack plane were revealed, which could be ready by the year 2012, coinciding with the finalization of the production of the A/B series.

An advanced aircraft

The design has the tails and the leading edges of the wings reduced to minimize the reflected signal and has a diamond

shape to hold greater quantities of fuel in its internal tanks. It incorporates a digital flight control system interconnected by fiber optics and has been produced using advanced materials (titanium, aluminium, carbon fibers, steel and thermoplastics) to guarantee the smallest radar signature. It has good aerodynamic qualities and to improve vision the air intakes have been set back with the pilot's position further forward. The F-22A has been created to dominate the air space of the 21st century.

It is fitted out with two Pratt & Whitney F-11-PW-100 jet engines with 15,890 kg of thrust, which have two dimensional nozzles with the capability of directing the exhaust

MATERIAL
The construction of an aircraft capable of eluding enemy radars demands the use of particular design techniques with the use of composite and absorption materials which reduce the signature and absorb the waves hitting the «Raptor».

«SPIRIT OF AMERICA»
Presented in public on the 6th of March 1997, the «spirit of America» is the first production unit of the advanced stealth fighter bomber the F-22 «Raptor» which is expected to be in service with the United States Air Force from the year 2000 to complement and substitute the older F-15 «Eagle».

jet at an angle between +/- 20 degrees, enjoying great maneuverability at the same time as reaching a supercruising velocity of Mach 1.58 without using re-heat. Two central computers- CIP's (Central Integrated Processors) co-ordinate the work of the sensors, link together the sophisticated avionic equipment and have the responsibility for managing the aircraft's flight at the same time as communicating with the radar to fully exploit its navigation and air-to-air combat capabilities.

This is utilized to launch weapons, housed in three internal bays to reduce the radar signature, such as short range Sidewinder infra red missiles, medium-range AMRAAM radar-guided missiles and 454 kg bombs among others, with a maximum load of 2,268 kg.

Designed to shoot down short, medium and long-range aircraft, they constitutes the main offensive components in air-to-air combat missions and are in a constant state of evolution to face threats which constantly change in character. They are used across a wide range of fighters and are optional in training, transport and specialist, aircraft, offering both a defensive and offensive capability.

Development

The need to shoot down other enemy aircraft during the first world war led to the machine gun being adopted as an offensive weapon. When this was demonstrated to be inadequate, it was substituted by many kinds of cannons. The performance of these and the changing nature of the threats led to various developments, such as the X-4 guided missile, which didn't reach production, developed by Dr Kramer in the Ruhrstahl factory at the end of the second world war. Then there were the 2.75" rockets used by the United States up to the middle of the 1950's which crystallized from the studies carried out by the United States Navy Bureau of Aeronautics to be supplied with a missile capable of shooting down airplanes flying at Mach 1.

The guided missile
Managed by McDonnell Douglas, the development took components from a naval anti-aircraft missile designed earlier and incorporated a radar guidance system which was finally evaluated in the Mugu Point Missile Validation Center in California. Produced since 1951 under the name Sparrow Model 1, its inadequate performance led to further alternative research programs by Raytheon and McDonnell, which ended up with the N-6 version of the missile. It entered service in 1958 in the F-38 «Demon» fighters.

In parallel to this development work engineers from the company Philco were working on the development of a missile which incorporated a five-inch non-guided rocket with a special head for hunting targets. After the first launches in 1953, the Sidewinder was ready three years later and in 1958 brought down its first aircraft in the Formosa crisis. A conflict in which a missile was fired against a Chinese aircraft which did not explode, remaining stuck in its fuselage. Shortly afterwards a Soviet copy appeared called the AA-2 «Atoll»

brought about after a detailed study of the captured United States weapon.

Weapon developments

The need to provide fighter aircraft with all kinds of particular missiles led to the beginning of the development of weapons such as the United States Bell Eagle, Hughes Falcon , Grumman Phoenix and the Soviet AA-1 Alkali, AA-3 Anab, AA-4 Awl, AA-5 Ash. The necessities brought about by the Vietnam conflict led to the introduction of much-improved and more capable missiles than before, at the same time that aircraft performance advanced in maximum speed, maneuverability, and the power of the on-board radars.

The design of a new generation of fighter bombers brought about the creation of missiles capable of carrying out quicker maneuveres and reaching their targets from

ASRAAM

Created as a substitute for the «Sidewinder» and backed by British industry, the short range infra-red ASRAAM missile has been subjectes to many flights and trial firings to prove is capability before being put into service in 1998 with the Harrier GR7 and Eurofighter 2000.

MICA

The French industry continues its success in its development of advanced products such as the MICA which incorporates a version guided by radar, and is equipped with an infra-red self guidance system (see photograph to the right).

SELF DEFENCE

Helicopters have been given the capability to face similar aircraft with the provision of light air- to-air missiles such as these French ATAM Mistral missiles.

greater distances. Therefore the French created the Matra Magic and R530; the British the Red Top and Sky Flash; the Italian the Aspide, and the Israelis the Shafir, which have been kept hidden with new variants and more advanced models continuing up to the present day. At a time when aerial combat involves the use of a combination of airborne radar warning systems, communication, management and control in real

time, reconnaissance and detection satellites, and components reducing signatures based on Stealth technology etc, missiles continue evolving to face ever more complex and capable threats. Some of these are detailed in the following section.

Infra-red Advances

This relies on a sensor in the guidance head of the missile to lock onto the target, and includes a rocket engine with fixed or vectoral thrust to arrive at the target area and impact with it. It relies on fins and a very sleek fuselage to get the necessary flight sta-

western fighters defence over short distances in the majority of occidental fighters. With more than 150,000 units produced and different countries manufacturing it under licence, the Sidewinder has proven its effectiveness in the aerial conflicts such as the Falklands and Gulf wars with the more advanced L (or LI Improved), M, P, &X Evolved Sidewinder versions.

Similar to this is the French Magic, the latest being version 2 which has capabilities in every aspect with great maneuverability and the capability of being fired during any of the flight maneuveres of the host aircraft, giving it enough features to satisfy the widest range of combat necessities.

bility, and maneuverability allowing it to bring down the aircraft being attacked.

In the lower segment of this category are the United States FIM-92 «Stinger»AA, the Russian SA-18 Grouse, the British Starstreak and the French ATAM, a particular version of the Mistral. These were created for attack helicopters and airplanes in slow flight doing transport or reconnaissance

A wide spectrum

Derived, in more or less the same size as earlier models, from those which in some

work, giving them a real air-to-air self-defence capability against similar aircraft. The mode of operation is the type "fire and forget" with the tracking head locked onto the target until it reaches it.

The «Sidewinder»

With a greater range and size than the others mentioned, multiple designs have been created following from the Hughes Sidewinder of the United States, it guarantees a kill over short distances with most

cases have taken advantage of components or highly evolved characteristics we find the advanced Rafael Shafir 2, and Python 3- responsible for shooting down 50 Syrian aircraft in the Bekaa Valley. Also the Israeli Python 4, the Chinese CATIC PL-5, PL-7, PL-8, PL-9 which appear to be similar to the designs of other countries. There is also the Bra-

ZH590

INFRA-RED MISSILES

DESIGNATION	ORIGIN	RANGE	MECHANISM	WEIGHT	EXPLOSIVE HEAD
MAA-1	Brazil	5 km	Active laser	90 kg	12 kg HE (*) fragmented
PL-9	China	5 km	Active laser	120 kg	10 kg HE
R-550 Magic 2	France	5 km	Radio frequency	90 kg	13 kg HE fragmented
MICA IR	France	50 km	Active radar	110 kg	12 kg HE fragmented
Python 4	Israel	15 km	Active laser	105 kg	11 kg HE fragmented
ASRAAM	G. Britain	15 km	Active laser	87 kg	HE fragmented
IRIS-T	Germany	12 km	Active laser	87 kg	11,4 kg HE fragmented
U-DARTER	S. Africa	8 km	Active laser	95 kg	17 kg HE fragmented
AIM-9X «Sidewinder»	USA	10 a 15 km	Combined	84 kg	10 kg HE fragmented
AA-8 «Aphid»	Russia	3-5 km	Radar or active laser	65 kg	6 kg HE fragmented
AA-10 «Alamo»	Russia	40 o 70 km	Active radar	254 or 350 kg	39 kg
AA-11 «Archer»	Russia	20 o 30 km	Active radar	105 or 110 kg	7,4 kg HE fragmented

* HE, High Explosive

The soviet surprise

The characteristics of the Vimpel AA-11 Archer missile caused a great stir in the West, equipping Russian designed aircraft, of which Germany has a group which made up a part of the MiG-29 arsenal of the old Democratic Republic. With a tracker capable of locking onto targets located at 45 degrees to its axis at a range of 30 km. With excellent maneuverability resulting from the vectoral thrust of its propulsion unit, it can hit targets when turning at 12 g's. It is much more advanced than was initially believed and sails past its western equivalents in terms of performance.

Future reply

To counteract it advanced designs such as the Matra Bae Dynamics ASRAAM (Advanced Short Range Air-to-Air Missile) have been worked on, which incorporates a tracker refrigerated by argon and nitrogen, is very resistant to counter measures, and has a long-range detection capability. There is also the German Bodenseewerk Geratetechnik IRIS-T with outstanding range and maneuverability and the French Matra MICA which combines a highly efficient combat missile head, an advanced

zilian Sistemas Aeroespaciasis MAA-1 Piranha and the South African Kukry, Darter and U-Darter which will include vectoral thrust and a focal plane array tracker which distinguish between thermal images generated by the target and the background, being much more selective in the area chosen.

propulsion unit giving it a range of 50 km and, depending on the mission, the possibility of mounting an infra-red sensor or radar guidance unit.

Radar guidance

With a longer range than earlier versions, occasionally exceeding 100 km, capable of managing significant changes in altitude, a cruising speed greater than Mach 3, and a radar tracker incorporated in the guidance unit; these missiles are aimed at intercepting medium and long-range targets.

Made in the USA and spread throughout the world, the AIM-7 Sparrow being used at the moment corresponds to the versions F,M & P, provided with a monopulse, semi-

GUIDED MISSILES

DESIGNATION	ORIGIN	RANGE	MECHANISM	WEIGHT	EXPLOSIVE HEAD
PL-11	China	25 km	—	220 kg	HE fragmented
MICA AR	France	50 km	Active radar	110 kg	12 kg HE fragmented
Aspide	Italy	40 km	Active radar	220 kg	30 kg HE fragmented
AIM-7P «Sparrow»	USA	45 km	Active radar	230 kg	39 kg HE fragmented
AIM-120 «AMRAAM»	USA	50 km	Active radar	157 kg	22 kg HE direct fragmentation
AA-9 «Amos»	Russia	100 km	Active radar	490 kg	47 kg HE fragmented
AA-12 «Adder»	Russia	50 km	Active laser	175 kg	30 kg HE fragmented
R-37	Russia	150 km	—	600 kg	60 kg HE fragmented

active radar tracker, improved resistance to electronic counter measures and in the case of the M & P a fragmentation explosive head. Originating from this missile are the Italian Alenia IDRA/Aspide Mk2, the British BAE Sky Flash and various Chinese copies somewhat larger, designated PL-10 & PL-11 manufactured by CATIC, with the French counterpart being the Matra Super 530D.

The Hughes AIM-120 AMRAAM (Advanced Medium Range Air-to-Air Missile), guided by active radar, is the logical evolution from the Sparrow, with a range of 50 km and supplied with substantially improved electronics to face the threats forecast for the beginning of the 21st century. With an updated capability the Hughes AIM-54C+ is the most advanced version of the Phoenix which operates in conjunction with the F-14 Tomcat, guided by radar with a range of 150 km.

Faced with the varied number of weapons offered by Occidental countries, Russia has made great efforts to provide its

fighters, and those units for export, with a very wide range of missiles designed with a high level of performance. Among these are the particularly noteworthy AA-5 Acrid R-46, AA-7 Apex R-24R, AA-8 Aphid R-60, AA-9 Amos R-33 and its advanced R-37 version destined for the MiG-31 interceptor Foxhound, AA-1 Alamo R-27 in configurations which reach distances between 40 and 110 km, AA-12 Adder or R-77 AMRAAMSKI, and the AAM-L which can reach objectives located 400 km away.

SUPER «SIDEWINDER»

The Hughes AIM-9X is the United States industry's answer to the requirements of the US Navy for a short-range infra-red missile with an advanced tracking head, with control components which give it greater maneuverability, and a rocket engine with enough power to follow every kind of target.

OPERATION

With self protection infra-red missiles on the extremities of the wings which allow it to confront similar missiles, this Mirage F-1 is ready to begin a ground bombing mission.

ADVANCED

The latest version of the Mirage 2000 to enter service was model 5 which incorporated an improved attack and navigation system combined with a new pilot aircraft interface, RDY doppler radar, integrated counter measure system, firing capability against various targets at the same time and the possibility of using a wide range of air-to-air and air-to-surface weapons.

Following the tradition of earlier fighters, beginning with the Mirage III and F-1. The Mirage 2000 advanced fighter bomber was created as a more economical reply to the cancelled ACF project. It was designed to satisfy the needs of the L'Armee de L'Air and to guarantee the manufacturing independence of the French aeronautical industry. Widely spread throughout those countries which buy French military products, this fighter bomber has maintained a healthy manufacturing capability which makes France the third largest exporter of arms in the world.

Development of the Mirage 2000

Continuing with the proven design ideas of the delta wing Mirage III, V and 5/50, the designer Marcel Bloch, put his design philosophy into the development of this multi-purpose fighter, which gave it significantly more advanced qualities than earlier French models. Which although gaining outstanding sales success, showed themselves to be inferior to their comparable United States aircraft both in capability and reliability.

Development

After the cancellation of the ACF (Avion du Combat Futur) project for budgetary reasons, the development of a new combat aircraft to substitute it began in 1973. Since the mid 1980's the aircraft in

the service of the French Air Force were manufactured by the company Dassault Aviation, centralizing the country's aircraft manufacturing capability.

The inaugural flight for the first of these took place at the Istres base on the 10th of March 1976. The fourth with a shorter tail was flown in May 1980, and the twin-seater in October of the same year. In parallel to these processes, there was from 1979 the production of a version specifically aimed at nuclear penetration, which flew on the 2nd of February 1983. On the 24th of October 1990 the multi-purpose 2000-5 was ready, being the latest model of this design,

USERS	
MODEL	**COUNTRIES (No of units)**
2000B	Egypt (4), France (30), Greecce (4)
2000C	France (124)
2000N	France (75)
2000D	France (86)
2000DAD/DP	Abu Dhabi (6), Peru (2)
2000E	Abu Dhabi (22), Egypt (16), Greecce 36
2000H	India (42)
2000P	Peru (10)
2000RAD	Abu Dhabi (8)
2000TH	India (7)
2000-5	France (37), updated from earlier versions
2000-5E	Qatar (9), Taiwan (48)
2000-5D	Qatar (3), Taiwan (12)
Various	7 prototypes and 6 production units used by Dassault as demonstration aircraft.

incorporating noteworthy advances over earlier versions already in service.

Deliveries

22 aircraft were ordered as a result of the French defence budget in 1980, the first of which was destined for the l'Armee de l'Air and flew on the 20th of November 1982. The first operational squadron was formed on the 2nd of July 1984, when the EC 1/2 Cigognes from the Dijon-Longvic base reached the level required, with these aircraft being successfully used in the air-to-air and air-to-surface missions assigned to them.

Later, overseas orders arrived and the first operational squadron was announced in 1985. After this, orders for 550 aircraft arrived for all of the versions from the air forces of eight countries, half way through 1997 450 of these had been delivered.

> **CAPABLE**
>
> Designed to face multiple threats in an airspace saturated with electronic counter measures, the twin-seater D version incorporates a nozzle for in flight refueling and can be equipped with a laser illuminator to guide its 1,000 kg BGL Arcole laser bombs until they hit their target.

Going for a multi-purpose aircraft

After adapting the initial concept from being purely an interceptor to one with a more multi-purpose role to include ground attacks, the Mirage 2000 has demonstrated that it is capable of successfully carrying out multiple combat missions. These including long distance interception, aerial superiority, long-range penetrations, exclusion missions for enemy forces, attacking targets of great importance, the neutralization of air bases with anti-runway weapons, the control of naval vessels, reconnaissance, and tactical & strategic nuclear attack.

2000C TECHNICAL CHARACTERISTICS

COST:	34,5 million dollars	PROPULSION:	
DIMENSIONS:		A SNECMA M53-P2 jet engines with 9.690 kg of thrust.	
Length	14.16 m	**PERFORMANCE:**	
Height	5.2 m	Ceiling service height	16,460 m
Wingspan	9.13 m	High altitude speed	+ Mach 2.2
Wing surface area	41 m²	Low altitude speed	Mach 0.9
WEIGHTS:		Approach speed	259 km/h
Empty	7,500 kg	Runway length	457 m
Maximum	17,000 kg	Interceptor range	1,480 km
Max. external load	6,300 kg	Extended range	3,333 km
Internal fuel load	3,978 kg	Design load factor	+ 9 g
External fuel load	4,700 kg		

The capability of the Mirage 2000

The Mirage 2000 program has been able to maintain the French aeronautical industry as an international force conserving the important market share which it has traditionally occupied.

Equipment

The pilot sits on an Martin-Baker F-10Q ejector seat, manufactured in France under license. He has at his disposition a fly-by-

wire digital electronic flight control system, relying on the support of the SFENA autopilot with an advanced cockpit allowing him to travel comfortably thanks to the ABG-Semca air-conditioning system. In addition he has the support of equipment such as the VOR/ILS Socrat 8900, the SAGEM Uliss 52 inertial system, the TRT radio altimeter system, V/UHF & UHF communication systems and the IFF CNI NRAI-7A/11 transponder-interrogator, with many of these linked by a 2084 XR digital bus. The first models included a Thomson-CSF RDM multi-mode radar and the latest rely on the Dassault Electronique/Thomson-CSF RDI Doppler pulse

radar, both of which have an estimated range of 100 kilometers and with a high capability of working in atmospheres saturated with electronic counter measures. The French versions N & D incorporate a radar 5 version specializing in terrain tracking with a cartographic mode of operation, two inertial navigators and a GPS satellite positioner.

Propulsion

It incorporates a SNECMA M53-P2 jet engine which has been demonstrated to be solid and powerful during its years in service. This aircraft is capable of flying at a speed of around Mach 1 at low altitude, reaching more than Mach 2 when flying at high altitude and

its acceleration capability is outstanding.

With 9,690 kg of thrust when using re-heat which is increased to 9,900 kg with the P20 version, and 6,500 kg when it is not used. It has a long operational range thanks to the fuel tank under the fuselage with a capacity of 2,498 liters and one under each wing with 1,480 liters. The twin seater has 74 liters less fuel.

Its weaponry

With nine fixing points, two on each wing and five on the fuselage, this aircraft can carry out both aerial defence and pre-cision attack missions. The single-seater

APACHE

The capability of operating with the stealth air to surface APACHE missile gives the Mirage 2000 greatly incre-ased potential allowing it to attack targets from a sufficiently safe dis-tance, avoiding the reaction of anti-aircraft defences. In addition it has two Magic 2 infra-red missiles to defend itself in the case of another aircraft trying to intercept it.

EQUIPMENT

The upper part of the tail incorporates a Thomson CSF Serval receiver warning about other radars and in the lower part there is a housing for a parachute to facilitate breaking (photograph to the right).

WEAPONRY

The different fixing points below the wings and fuselage allow it to carry out all kinds of missions, with Magic 2 missiles used in air to air missions and AS-30 laser guided missiles for ground attacks (photograph to the left).

has two 30 mm DEFA 554 cannons (which the twin-seater does not have); two short range Matra 550 infra-red missiles; Magic/Magic2 or MICA IR on the extreme sub wing fixings; four Matra Super 530F or MICA medium range laser-guided mis-siles located in the fixings below the air intakes on the fuselage.

A multi-purpose fighter

As a multi-purpose fighter principally destined for air-to-air missions, it is equipped with an advanced Thomson-CSF RDY multi-mode radar which is simultaneously capable of detecting 24 targets and following the 8 which are more hostile. It relies on an ICMS integrated electronic counter measure system which doesn't require external housings and has a notably advanced cockpit. This includes a head up and head low display (HUD/HLD) in which the pilot can verify the tactical situation; two lateral data displays. A central display where radar supplied data can be presented and a flight control system based on the HOTAS principle according to which the pilot selects nearly all of the command functions without having to take his hand off the joystick.

Its air-to-surface weaponry combines 250 kg free-fall bombs; laser guided 1,000 kg bombs; Durandal & BAP 100 anti-run-way bombs; Belouga submunitions dispensers; cruise & long range APACHE missiles; AS30L laser-guided & high precision missiles; Armat anti-radar missiles; anti-ship Exocets and in the nuclear penetration version N, the ASMP atomic warhead. The defensive system includes a Thomson-CSF Serval radar warner, an integrated counter measure system and a Alkan LL 5062 flare launcher.

The Mirage 2000-5

Recently put into production, the first aircraft of this model for France flew on the 26th of February 1996, Taiwan received its five units in April 1997, destined for the 2nd Tactical Fighter Wing. Qatar also gave an order, substituting them for its F-1's which Spain purchased. Doing so for a model combining up to date technological advances in its design, resulting in an advanced capability to face the threats of the next twenty years.

The advanced lightweight single seater MiG-29 was the Soviet response to the need for providing itself with a modern aircraft which could substitute in a favorable way the earlier generation and which would have the qualities necessary to face up to the latest United States designs, while at the same time constituting an interesting aircraft for other countries. Its capabilities and possibilities have meant that it will maintain itself as a product with a key export role up to the year 2005. The last of these produced for Russia itself was in 1991.

An adapted fighter

Its operational and technical requirements were created in the LFI document (Legkiy Frontovoy Istrebityel, a lightweight fighter for the front line) in 1972, with a view to replacing the MiG-21 & 23 and the Sukhoi 15 & 17, but it wasn't until 1974 that the order to build it came. The first of 13 prototypes flew from the Ramenskoye base on the 6th of October 1977 and was caught by United States spy satellites the following month, it was baptized in the West as RAM-L.

MiG-29 in service

A second aircraft was ready in June 1978, although like a quarter of the aircraft destined for evaluation it crashed due to engine failure. The production of the new model was begun in 1982 at the MAPO (Moscow Aircraft Production Organisation) factories. The following year delive-

> **GERMAN**
> The re-unification of Germany has meant that the Luftwaffe is operating a total of 23 MiG-29's, employed for both combat and training exercises, unlike other NATO countries.

> **CAPABILITY**
> Designed to face the threat of Occidental designs during the 1970's, the MiG -29 has been built as an advanced fighter bomber capable of conquering world markets.

ries to squadrons began, in 1985 it was considered to be operational and in July 1986 it could be seen in public for the first time when six of them flew at an exhibition in Finland. This allowed it to be examined up close for its flight agility and capability to be checked out.

The Fulcrum A, project 9.12, corresponds to the first version produced with three sub-types differentiated by small changes in some of the external details, while the B version, project 9.51, is a twin-seater trainer with total combat capability although it lacks radar. After its first flight on the 4th of May 1984, work began on the C type which has greater curvature where the fuselage joins with the cockpit, the aim being to carry more electronic equipment, possibly taken from other areas, improving the fuel load capacity by 75 liters, which in the original was significantly less.

Use with aircraft carriers

The K version identified as Korabelny began production in November 1989, which was to be flown exclusively from aircraft carriers. The extremities of the wings can be folded; it uses special RD-22K jet engines relies on a Zhuk radar. It has a greater fuel load and can carry various weapons some of the more notable ones being the Kripton AS-17 anti-ship missile.

Export possibilities

Advanced versions of the type C aircraft, with the designation S, have been produced since 1992 to improve export possibilities. With SD, SE & SM subversions this model includes digital flight controls;

DESIGN
The MiG-29's aerodynamics and mission capability have brought about great manufacturing success with exports to more than twenty countries, with Peru being the last to receive some.

AGILITY
The design, engine power and general mission capabilities allow this Russian fighter bomber to fight other Occidental designs in air-to-air missions from an advantageous position, enjoying a good reputation among its users.

missiles, including the SD's destined for Malaysia's MiG-29N. Adaptations for its use in tropical countries; satellite communication and navigation equipment; in-flight refueling system allowing it to receive 900 liters per minute; internal fuel tanks with 1,500 additional liters; structural improvements which allow it 28 degree attack angles compared with 22 degrees in the original; a RD-22 series 3 engine with a planned life-span of 2,000 hours.

Improved avionics

In the 1997 Salon Le Bourget a new configuration was presented with improved avionics, including four multi-function display screens- two large and two small for data

two multi-function display screens; a cockpit lengthened by 20 centimeters; eight sub-wing fixing points; and various modifications to the structural configuration for it to carry more fuel. A modernized Sapfir N019 (RP-29) radar with the capability of following two fighters at the same time (not just one as with the earlier versions); an updated Ts101M weapons computer; the possibility of employing more advanced

ters. Six hundred of these form a part of the Russian Air Force, with exports to some 24 countries to which Israel must be added, which has purchased some for pilot training purposes, and the United States which has recently ordered 21 units .

This outstanding sales success is due in part to Russian sales policies and the good capability of the airplane, which can carry out many different kinds of missions and

presentation. Conventional instrumentation in a smaller size; a Topaz N019M radar provided with a terrain following mode and resolution of 15m; the possibility of employing AS-14 Kedge and AS-17 missiles, the first for surface attack and the second for anti-ship attack with active radar.

Sales success

Initially produced in the Znamya Truda and Nizhny Novgorod factories under the tutelage of MAPO, some 1,500 units have been built of which two hundred are UB twin-sea-

which requires less maintenance than other earlier designs. Despite having a small radius of action, relying on antiquated equipment and having been designed without considering the reduction of the radar signature, among its virtues are its maneuverability and agility in combat; excellent performance during slow flight; good visibility for the pilot who sits on a K-36DM ejector, inclined at an angle of 10 degrees helping him in the fast maneuveres which take place in close aerial combat and the acceleration of the two engines.

These engines consume a significant quantity of fuel and emit black fumes which are visible over a long distance. They are RD-33 jet engines produced by Klimov/Sarkisov and are fed by large nozzles designed to guarantee the greatest flow of air at any speed, although their low position has necessitated the incorporation of a mechanical system, to close them when taxiing to avoid taking in foreign bodies which could cause damage.

In September 1996 a MiG-29 was displayed at the Farnborough Air Show in Britain supplied with RD-133 vectoral thrust engines, which thanks to nozzle movement in three directions gives it gre-

WEAPONRY

GSh-301 Cannon	Very lightweight 30 mm caliber and with a capacity 150 shells.
KAB-500KR Bombs	Guided by television
BKF & ZAP-500 Bombs	Free fall. The first are high explosive and the second are Napalm incendiary bombs.
B-8M1 & S-24B launchers	These are for 80 and 240 mm rockets respectively.
AA-8 Aphid & AA-11 Archer	For use in air to air, short range and infra-red guided mission.s
AA-10A Alamo missiles	For use in air to air, medium range and radar guided missions.
AA-9 Amos missiles	For use in air to air, long range and radar guided missions.
AS-14 Kedge missiles	For use against surface targets.
AS-17 Krypton A y P missiles	Used against ships at sea and for anti-radar work respectively. It incorporates a search radar.

ater agility and increased potential for the future.

In combat

During the Gulf War various Iraqi aircraft of this model confronted their western equivalents and suffered serious losses despite the pilots having red HMS displays incorporated in their helmets, these being very efficient and useful in close combat.

Although the cockpit is not ergonomic or comfortable, it can carry a wide range of weapons consisting of a cannon, different bombs & missiles supported by the capability of the OEPS-29 infra-red tracker which has a range of 15 km, which is integrated in the front of the cockpit; the Doppler impulse RLS RP-29 radar which has the capability to follow and attack targets flying below it, locating its targets within a radius of 100km and is equipped with a laser rangefinder. Despite these qualities, reports sent out by German pilots who have flown them mention the lack of power and the complicated handling.

> **COMBAT**
> Used by the Iraqis in Operation Desert Storm the MiG-29 could not show its qualities before the powerful Occidental war machine which was spread across the zone.

How it's equipped

With a Hydromash retractable under carriage and a body constructed from lightweight materials such as aluminium, carbon fiber, lithium and titanium, its equipment includes an integrated communication system with IFF detection; SRZ-15 interrogator and R-862 radio; INS navigation assistance; TACAN and GPS satellite positioning; self-protection system with a SPO-15LM radar threat warner; SO-69 transponders and a BVP-30-26M launcher for 26 decoy flares.

In addition the mission control system which has various computers linked with the radar, laser rangefinder, infra-red sensor and helmet designator, gives it capabilities which assure the destruction of every kind of aerial target at distances between 200 meters and 60 kilometers.

> **OPERATIONAL**
> The technology applied by Russia in aeronautical manufacture has substantially improved the operational level of its aircraft, which have demonstrated that they are capable of landing on foreign bases without excessive support or specific maintenance equipment.

VERSION C TECHNICAL CHARACTERISTICS

COST:	28 million dollars		External fuel load	2,200 kg
DIMENSIONS:			**PROPULSION:**	TWO KLIMOV/SARKISOV RD-33
Length	17.32 m			JET ENGINES WITH 8,290 KG OF THRUST EACH.
Height	4.73 m		**PERFORMANCE:**	
Wingspan	11.36 m		Ceiling service height	17,000 m
Wing surface area	38 m²		High altitude speed	Mach 2.3
WEIGHTS:			Low altitude speed	Mach 1.06
Empty	10,900 kg		Runway length	250 m
Maximum	18,500 kg		Interception range	600 km
Maximum external load	3,000 kg		Extended range	2,900 km
Internal fuel load	4,500 kg		Design load factor	9 g

PROPULSION UNITS

Located between the two vertical tails are the Klimov/Sarkisov RD-33 jet engines with 8,290 kg of thrust each, giving it great agility, although with a high fuel consumption it has a reduced range.

SUB WING

Sub-wing and fuselage fixing points allow it to carry a reduced payload, put at around two tonn. This is an aspect which has been substantially improved in the latest versions increasing this capacity up to four tons.

UNDER CARRIAGE

The under carriage is a solid construction allowing it to operate from semi-prepared grass runways, improving its capability to make landings in the most difficult combat conditions.

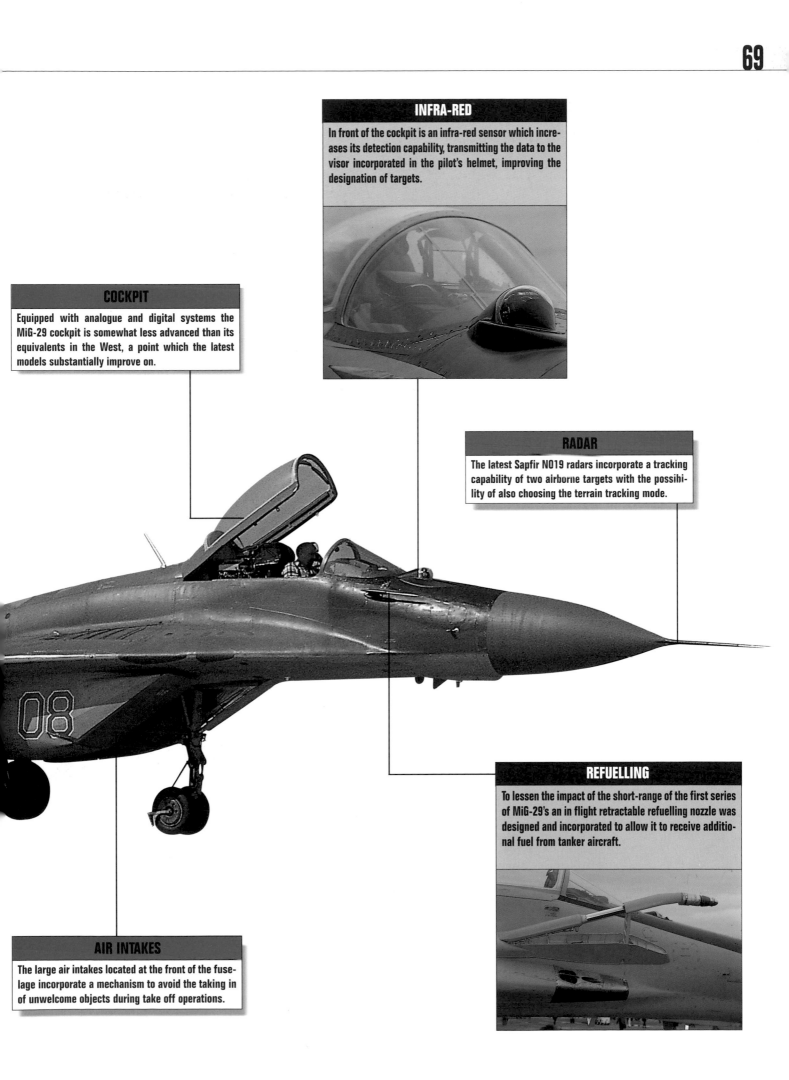

INFRA-RED

In front of the cockpit is an infra-red sensor which increases its detection capability, transmitting the data to the visor incorporated in the pilot's helmet, improving the designation of targets.

COCKPIT

Equipped with analogue and digital systems the MiG-29 cockpit is somewhat less advanced than its equivalents in the West, a point which the latest models substantially improve on.

RADAR

The latest Sapfir NO19 radars incorporate a tracking capability of two airborne targets with the possibility of also choosing the terrain tracking mode.

REFUELLING

To lessen the impact of the short-range of the first series of MiG-29's an in flight retractable refuelling nozzle was designed and incorporated to allow it to receive additional fuel from tanker aircraft.

AIR INTAKES

The large air intakes located at the front of the fuselage incorporate a mechanism to avoid the taking in of unwelcome objects during take off operations.

STEALTH

Created as the result of the application of the most advanced techniques of invisibility, the B-2 combines great potential for applications both in the carrying out of conventional attack missions and in its use as a strategic weapon of mass destruction with nuclear weapons.

After the huge bombing operations of cities and strategic targets carried out during the Second World War, the Korean, and Vietnam Wars. It seemed that technological advances were going to be paramount in the search for aircraft capable of carrying out precision attacks instead of saturation bombing. This was not the case, and the United States Government encouraged the manufacture of a series of models which included the General Dynamics F-111 Aardvark and the B-1B Lancer and B-2 Spirit Bombers. Meanwhile various up-dates were programmed for the B-52 fleet with a view to maintaining the Strategic Air Command's (SAC) deterrence and penetration capability.

WINGS

During the labors of taking off and landing in which it is flown at low speed , the B-1B requires additional lift. This is increased by varying the angle of the wings until they are located at their most forward position.

Supported in nearly twenty bases and with its own training area designated SRTC (Strategic Range Training Complex) which depends on the Strategic Weapons School (SWS), at the moment SAC units consist of aircraft in the following roles: RC-135 strategic reconnaissance & electronic; KC-135 & KC-10 in-flight refueling; E-4B aerial management & control; B-52's version G & H with seventy aircraft in service; B-1B & B-2. We are going to analyze the last two with respect to their capability and modernity.

The Rockwell B-1B Lancer

In 1962 research began on a low altitude strategic penetration bomber which would substitute the B-52 in the 1980's. In November 1969 the requirements were sent out to the industry and in June 1970 the proposal by North American Rockwell was taken on.

LIGHTWEIGHT

Employed in light bombing missions in which it stands out for the load it can carry and the possibility of varying the angle of its wings, the F-111 is at this moment carrying out missions related with electronic warfare.

The prototypes

With five prototypes ordered, later reduced to four, manufacturing work took place in the Palmdale factory in California, and the first flight was carried out on the 23rd of December 1974. After the cancellation of the initial project by President Carter, President Reagan authorized the manufacture of a hundred B-1B aircraft in October 1981, including various modifications with respect to the original model, having detected some flaws in the design.

Incorporation

The first unit flew on the 18th of October 1984 and the second on the 4th of May 1985 destined for the 96th bomber wing at Dyess base in Texas. The last was manufactured on the 20th of January 1988 with all of them being equipped at the Dyess, Ellsworth, Grand Forks and McConnel bases

TRIAD

The combination of B-52 G/H, B-1B & B-2 bombers with around two hundred aircraft, constitutes a basic deterrence component for the United States Air Force, being employed in both conventional and nuclear type missions.

with some alternative deployments to other locations. Of these aircraft four were lost in various accidents and another two remain at Edwards Air force Base with the Air Force Systems Command (AFSC).

Since going into service various negative reports have come out relating to its capabilities, in particular its electronic self-protection system and the sealing of the fuel tanks. However, with time and large investments the initial defects have been rectified and now it is considered to be a an excellent aircraft for penetration and bombing at low altitude, for which it has been consigned the use of conventional weaponry.

Configuration

To develop the basic attack activity it was decided to design it following a classical configuration, but incorporating the best advances to increase its potential. At one end is the cockpit incorporating a front section where the pilot and co-pilot are located, including windscreens with detachable aluminium screens which protect them from the flash resulting from a nuclear explosion; advanced digital avionics and a rear section where two specialists in offensive and defensive weapons work; the four crew members have ACES II ejector seats at their disposition.

With computer controlled canards

located at the front below the cockpit to improve low altitude flight, the main characteristic is the inclusion of two stub wings with a variable angle, partly manufactured in 6AL-4V titanium alloy, to increase the aircraft's lift. This aspect is improved by moving the slats, activated hydraulically, to give greater wing curvature during maneuveres at low speed and with high angles of attack.

Capability

Four General Electric F101-GE-102 jet engines are located in two gondolas below the fixed wing section giving a thrust close to 55,000 kg, which is sufficient for bombing activities. Its bomb bay has a lot of capacity, housing three rotary launchers; there are eight fixing points below the fuselage where it is possible to put additional fuel tanks if required.

To support its activities it incorporates complex electronic self defence equipment consisting of 108 components, which is based on the AN/ALQ-161 system; the fixed inlet nozzles incorporate reflective screens which soften and reduce the radar signature produced, and also incorporates radar absorbing materials; the paintwork has been changed to a dark green/grey which reduces

INSTRUMENTATION

With analogue and digital controls, the B-1B bomber twin-seater cockpit has all the necessary components for its pilots to perform the flight and bombing operations in the most rational manner.

the infra-red signature. Additionally, it has satellite communication, an offensive ORS Westinghouse AN/APQ-164 radar; an inertial navigator for automatic terrain tracking; a doppler type Honeywell ASN-131 SPN/GEANS radar altimeter; optimized equipment for the future with the implementation of CMUP (Conventional Mission Upgrade Programme) which improves radar reliability. In parallel the communication system is being improved with the Rockeell Collins AN/ARC-210 and the electronic counter measures system with the integration of the IDECN RF system.

LANCER

The Lancer strategic bomber has enormous potential for use against all kinds of objectives, although the development of its electronic self-defence system continues to be a problem after 10 years in action.

The B-2A Spirit

President Clinton, surrounded in controversy with congress at the moment doesn't want to acquire more units other than those which, at this moment, guarantee national security. However, Congress has approved the investment of 331 million dollars more in the program, with the reality that the B-2A represents a notable advance with respect to earlier aircraft.

Its development

The secret program to construct an advanced bomber began in 1978 and in 1983 included the requirement for operating at low altitude. The Northrop Grumman Corporation was contracted for the manufacture of 6 trial units, which would then be transformed into operational aircraft, the first of these finished at the Palmdale factory on the 22nd of November 1988.

On the 17th of July the following year the first flight took place allowing aircraft to travel to Edwards Air base. The first refueling in flight was carried from a KC-10A on the 8th of November 1989 and the first part of the trials ended in 1990 after having carried out 67 hours of flying time in 16 flights.

On the 23 of October 1990 the second part of the trials began in which another aircraft participated. It wasn't until the 8th of June 1991 that the third aircraft flew which

LANDING CARRIAGE

Due to its large size and weight the B-1B has been provided with a very robust landing carriage with two wheels in the front carriages and four in each of the rear ones, allowing take offs and landings at maximum weight.

PROPULSION UNITS

The four F-101-GE-102 General Electric turbofan exhaust nozzles together produce 52,325 kilograms of thrust when employing post combustion. They are very big and located in pairs on both sides of the fuselage.

OPTIMIZATION

The need for flying low to make detection difficult forces designers to optimize the inlet nozzles for the B-1B's engines in such a way that allows both high and low altitude flight.

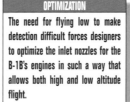

then included all the avionics, radar and other basic components. The fourth, fifth and sixth units were destined for weapon launching trials and operational testing.

The purchase

With an initial forecast of incorporating 133 B-2's, including the prototypes, cuts in 1991 reduced this total first to 76, then to 21 (the latest for conventional mission trials), this being the minimum number which the United States Air Force considered profitable to maintain. A good part of these has already been delivered to the 509 Bomber Wing at the Whiteman base in Missouri, supported by the Air Logistics Center (ALC) in Oklahoma. The first operational mission took place on the 4th of February 1996 with a take off in Guam.

However, all kinds of trials have been maintained with respect to capability and characteristic verification, including some carried out in 1997 resulting in IOC (Initial Operational Capability) certification. This was based on limited conventional operational capability after trials carried out at Nellis base, Las Vegas (Nevada) in which three B-2A aircraft destroyed 16 targets and also those carried out at the missile testing ground in White Sands, New Mexico where 16 JDAM (Joint Direct Attack

WEAPONRY

	B-1B LANCER	B-2A SPRIT
Capacity	60 tons of weapons	18 tons of weapons
Conventional attack	AGM-86B/C ALCM Missiles (Air Launched Cruise Missile) fitted with a conventional or submunition warhead, high explosive Mk84 907 kg or Mk82 227 kg free-fall bombs, Mk36 or Mk62 mines, cluster bombs with submunitions.	AGM-136 ACM Air Cruise Missiles &AGM137 -TSSAM (Tri-Service Standoff Attack Missiles) supplied with conventional or submunition warheads; Mk84 907 kg & Mk82 227 kg bombs; Mk 36 or Mk 62 mines; CBU 87/89/97/98 type cluster bombs with submunitions. At the moment the possibility of launching laser guided bombs is being worked on.
Nuclear attack	Abandoned at the moment, although its rotary launchers and fixing points can carry combinations of missiles: AGM-69A SRAM (Short-Range Attack Missile), AGM-86B/C ALCM missiles and B-61, B61-11 free-fall penetration bombs-tactical & strategic; B83 strategic bombs.	Cruise missiles and AGM-137 TSSAM missiles fitted with nuclear warheads and free fall bombs B-61, B61-11 & B83.

Munitions) were launched against 8 targets, hitting all of them.

An advanced bomber

Defined as a strategic penetration bomber, it incorporates substantial design advances to avoid being detected by enemy tracking radars, resulting in a high survival probability when carrying out combat missions. As a result a lot of work has been done to reduce its overall radar signature, based on a design which is very flat and with a minimum of vertical surfaces; the incorporation of advanced materials which absorb radar waves; the integration of the propulsion plant with the fuselage; and the adoption of measures for the reduction of the infra-red signature. Manufacture has followed strict computer control allowing precision machi-

DEVELOPMENT

Created as an advanced nuclear bomber, the B-1B has seen its missions develop to include precision attack with a variety of conventional weapons (photograph to the right).

ning of pieces to the order of 6.3 mm for the whole aircraft and the use of a special layer of paint/covering which recently is known to have suffered damage in flight. When operating in particular climatic conditions there are 80 hours of maintenance required for each one in the air.

PENETRATION

The design of the B-1B, the power of its engines and the capability of the subsystems allows the pilot to carry out penetration missions at low altitude making detection of the aircraft by enemy systems difficult. Actions where the radio altimeter and capability of varying the wing angle are basic.

Characteristics

The structure is a combination of materials such as aluminium, titanium, sandwich panels etc, in a way which has enabled the aircraft to be constructed with perfectly integrated rounded forms. The central section has the flight cockpit in the front part for two pilots with provision made for a third in the future if required. In the rear there are two weapon bays with rotary launchers in each of them. In the upper part of the fuselage is the receptacle for in flight refueling (using JP-8 fuel) which allows it to reach any part of the planet without needing to land.

On the sides there are two sections which each house two F118-GE-100 General Electric engines without re-heat, to make detection difficult, and which have a thrust of 8,125 kg each. Outside there are two arrow wings with an absorbent external edge and behind this an inverted double W shape incorporating the flaps which give the movement.

The internal equipment, the majority of which come under the classification secret, includes a band J AN/APQ-181 Hughes radar with 21 operation modes and has been designed as LPI (Low Probability of Intercept); a Tacan Rockwell-Collins TCN-250; GATS global positioning element (GPS-Aided Targeting System); Loral Federal AN/APR-50 RWR & Northrop Grumman ZSR-63 electronic support equipment; Milstar satellite communications.

Future forecasts are being changed radically for the time after the manufacturing process is finished in 1999. The units from numbers 1 to 16 form part of batch no 10, numbers 17 to 19 batch 20, the current standard batch 30, with expectations of introducing various modifications soon to the communications systems, navigation and weapons control. It is expected that operational readiness for this group of aircraft will be around the year 2000.

PENETRATION

Stealth B-2 bombers are considered to be aircraft with the greatest survival capability constructed to date and can be used in conventional and strategic missions against fixed and mobile targets.

TECHNICAL CHARACTERISTICS

	B-1B «LANCER»	B-2 «SPIRIT»				
COST:	200 million dollars	Between 1,000 & 2,000 million dollars	**Fuel**	88.450 kg	90.720 kg	
			Maximum take off weight	216.365 kg	170.550 kg	
DIMENSIONS:			**PROPULSION:**	Four General Electric F-101-GE-102 jet engines with re-heat giving a total of 52,325 kg of thrust.	Four General Electric F-118-GE-100 jet engines with out re-heat giving a total of 32,500 kg of thrust.	
Length	44,81 m	21,03 m				
Wingspan	23,84 m with wings folded 41,67 m with wings extended	52,43 m				
Height	10,36 m	5,18 m	**PERFORMANCE:**			
Wing surface area	181,2 m²	465,4 m²	**Maximum speed**	Mach 1.25	Mach 1	
WEIGHTS:			**Penetration speed**	965 km/h	Mach 1	
			Tactical flight	62 m from ground	—	
Empty	87.090 kg	49.900 kg	**Maximum range**	12.000 km	12.231 km	
Internal arms	34.019 kg	18.144 kg	**Ceiling service height**	18.000 m	15.240 m	
External arms load	26.762 kg	Not carried				

To satisfy the needs of combat pilots destined for the ten operational squadrons which make up the Spanish air defence potential (located at various air bases and equipped with some one hundred and eighty aircraft of the type Mirage F 1B/C/E/Q, McDonnell Douglas EF-18A/A+/B+ Hornet and RF-4C Phantom), continual planning with respect to preparation and training.

This consists of an initial phase of schooling and operational assignment such that, progressively, the level of preparation necessary to guarantee operational capability in missions assigned is reached. These

missions consisting of air-to-air, air-to-surface and tactical reconnaissance.

Equipment

To carry out basic activities the combat pilot has flight crew equipment at his disposal which gives complete security at the moment of carrying out the assigned mission and the guarantee necessary for survival in case of an accident.

The components

The equipment consists of leather boots, a fire-proof cotton suit, a Beaufort protection suit for those missions which have to be carried out over water, Garment Cutaway CSU-13B/P anti-gravity suit which, connected from below to the belt, has the job of exercising enough pressure necessary to maintain blood circulation during maneuveres at a high number of g's

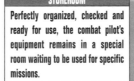

INSPECTION

Although aircraft are ready for use, the pilot always carries out an external inspection to check the state of various pieces of equipment and components. This work is supported by displays located on the fuselage.

STOREROOM

Perfectly organized, checked and ready for use, the combat pilot's equipment remains in a special room waiting to be used for specific missions.

- measuring the effort with respect to the force of gravity- and a flying hunter which offers protection against the cold.

In addition the pilots have at their disposal a Gentex Corporation HGU-55/P reduced-weight flight helmet with an interchangeable visor for daytime and nighttime flights; a Gentex MBU-12/P oxygen mask incorporating a microphone and green colored life jacket made in Britain. This is activated if the pilot finds himself in water, allowing him to keep his head clear, making it possible for him to breath without problems even if he has lost consciousness.

Survival equipment

The lifejacket pockets hold a number of items: a Sarbe 6 radio which is automatically activated at the moment of ejection, facilitating CSAR (Combat Search And Rescue) and which is powered by a long lasting lithium battery; flare signals and a useful

launcher; a stroboscope lamp; a military compass with tritium references allowing it to be used in any light conditions; a special key which opens the aircraft's inspection hatches in case it has to be repaired in a different base to normal.

Ejectable seat

All modern aircraft incorporate an ejection seat which allows the pilot a fast exit from the airplane (including when it is on the ground), thanks to a pyrotechnic system which explodes the canopy off (some seats smash it when going through) and retrorockets incorporated in the seat. In milliseconds the pilot is separated from the aircraft with parachutes then activated allowing to arrive on the ground without problems.

MISSION

The preparation of real missions is complex and requires the support of advanced computing systems which facilitate the preparation of the routes and the verification of calculations necessary to carry out flights, data which will be transferred onto the aircraft's computer.

COMPLET

The Spanish combat pilot's equipment combines all the necessary elements to carry out his activities and can be considered as one of the most modern of his generation (photograph to the right).

PREPARED

With the aircraft loaded with fuel, equipped with weapons and prepared to carry out its mission a pilot remains sitting in the cockpit waiting to receive the order to scramble (photograph to the left).

Kept below this seat is a survival kit which in the case of the Spanish F-18 Hornet aircraft is given the designation SKU-S/A and which stays fixed below the pilot

during the descent by parachute. This kit consists of a UHF radio beacon which emits at an emergency frequency facilitating the detection of the exact point of the crash. An additional life jacket; together withan automatically inflatable dingy; water and food to last for some time; coloring to

highlight the crash area on the sea; a dry sponge to soak up liquids; a whistle; sun screen to avoid sunburn; a survival and signal codes manual; a 15 m reel of fine &

MIRAGE

Installed in the small cockpit of the Mirage F-1C, a pilot from 141 squadron of the Albacete base is waiting to begin taxiing the runway before taking off and carrying out the assigned mission.

POST FLIGHT

With a video tape in his hand which has recorded flight images and data, a pilot from squadron 153 is discussing with a ground mechanic various aspects of the flight just carried out. The cassette will allow an analysis of the mission and correction of any deficiencies.

strong nylon; goggles; flares; an isothermic blanket; desalination tablets to allow the drinking of sea water and survival packs no.1 & 2 which include other complementary elements and medical equipment.

The pilots assigned to the Icarus Detachment in Bosnia, carrying out real missions launching weapons against ground targets carry in addition a Global Positioning System (GPS) from the United States company Magellan; a 9 mm Parabellum flare gun with a maximum capacity of 16 cartridges; an Air Force Aitor knife with a saw and blade; a map of the operational area; a guide for pronunciation of Yugoslavian languages; a black woollen cap and gloves; United States and German money which can be used to bribe the natives for until they arrive at a safe place; a I.D. card which identifies them as people assigned to missions for the United Nations Organisation (UNO); a AN/PRC-12 radio which allows listening and transmission; a Mini Maglite torch; water and high energy level chocolate bars.

Training

The preparation process for pilots is very similar to comparable western countries and is begun with exams for men and women between 19 and 22 years old who

have passed university entrance exams organized by the ministry of defence.

Entry

After passing the entry exams in which basic knowledge levels are evaluated along with physical capability, the aspiring pilots are subjected to both a complete physical and psychological medical examination. This is followed by difficult exams in mathematics, physics & chemistry. Those selected go forward to complete a specific training program at the General Air Academy located on the Menor Seashore inside the

PLANNING

Before executing pre-determined exercise the pilots meet in the operations room to analyze and co-ordinate various aspects of the task to be carried out.

SIMULATOR

In addition to carrying out the greatest number of flying hours possible, combat squadrons make use of advanced simulators which allow different kinds of exercises to be carried out.

premises of the San Javier Air Base, the courses last three years for those assigned to Air Operations in the middle scale and five years for those in the top section.

Preparation

Students receive a specific grounding through studying 67 complementary subjects, with practical flying lessons at the same time. Those aspiring to the top level begin the process in their third year with a single propeller E.26 Tamiz, the Spanish designation for the Chilean T-35 Pillan, manufactured under licence. In the fourth they fly with the E.25 Aviojet or CASA C-101 and in the fifth year, if they have been selected for it, specific combat training at the Fighter & Attack School of the Talavera 23rd Wing which some strengthen further with the Undergraduate Pilot Training program of the United States Air Force.

Destination

Once they have been given the rank Lieutenant or Second Lieutenant from the top and middle schools respectively, they can choose a place in different combat squadrons according to the results they

achived. After completing an operational conversion course for the Mirage F-1, F-18 Hornet or RF-4 Phantom, the pilots receive the LCR (Limited Combat Ready) qualification allowing them to carry out limited combat missions. This conversion course involves theoretical classes and flights in the most varied of atmospheric conditions, weapon-launching and the use of specific simulators allowing them to practice every kind of incident without risk to the aircraft. Now fully integrated in the squadrons they will complete basic complementary training which will lead them to being designated CR1 (Combat Ready 1) and later CR2 & CR3 reaching at this moment the highest level of preparation as combat pilots.

BIPLAZAS

Those aspiring pilots in the middle scale carry out a similar process, but in three years beginning flying lessons in the second year and completing their specialization in the third.

SPANISH COMBAT AVIATION

AIR BASE	UNIT	AIRCRAFT	MISSIONS
Manises in Valencia	11th Wing with 111 squadron	14 Mirage, type C/E & Q in modernization process	Air defence and surface attack
Los Llanos in Albacete	14th Wing with 141&142 squad	Thirty Mirage F-1 type B/C/E in modernization process	Air defence, surface attack, operational conversion.
Gando in Las Palmas de Gran Canaria	462 squadron with aircraft of the 14th wing	Fourteen Mirage F-1 type C/E in modernization process	Air defence, naval target attack, destruction of ground targets
Zaragoza	15th Group with 151, 152 & 153 squadron	34 EF-18A/B+ Hornets	Air-to-air combat, anti-aircraft defence submission, ground target attack, operational conversion.
Torrejón in Madrid	12th Wing with 121, 122 & 123 squadron	36 EF-18 A/B+ Hornets & 14 RF-4C Phantoms	Air-to-air combat, naval target attack, ground reconnaissance
Morón in Sevilla	Ala 121 con Escuadrón 211	Thirty EF-18 A/B in delivery process	Air-to-air combat and surface attack
Talavera La Real in Badajoz	Ala 23	Thirty modernized F-5B's.	Laser designation & surface attack.

nitially designed as an attack aircraft capable of counteracting ground threats resulting from a possible large scale attack by Warsaw Pact forces, the existing Tornado is a model which has evolved with various versions with great potential for the execution of air-to-air and air-to-surface tasks.

In this last activity it has been demonstrated as one of the most capable aircraft in existence at the moment being responsible for a great part of the low altitude missions during the first phases of the Desert Storm operation in the Gulf War.

GR4
With the capability of flying at very low altitude in any atmospheric condition, the GR4 improves penetration and attack capability compared with earlier models, with the result that the British Air Force has ordered the conversion of 142 units to this standard. It is forecast that these will be delivered between 1998 and 2002.

MULTI-NATIONAL
Coming from a multi-national program, the Tornado is an excellent precision attack aircraft with a large part of the British IDS units being programmed for modernization to the improved GR4 version.

A multi-national aircraft

The development of the Tornado began half way through the 1960's in the core of the North Atlantic Treaty Organisation (NATO) with the idea of providing an aircraft capable of carrying precision attacks, which would fly at low altitude to avoid being detected by enemy radar and shot down by anti-aircraft systems. On this premise, the 17th of July 1968 feasibility studies began encompassing the governments of Italy, Germany, Great Britain, Belgium, Canada and the United States with, in the end, the first three countries continuing with the project. The development phase was completed in July 1970 and the structural design in August 1972.

The first of the nine evaluation prototypes flew on the 14th of August 1974 and two years later, on the 29th of July, the governments involved in the aircraft purchase signed the production order for a total of 809 aircraft, these which would be divided into 6 batches, including the 6 pre-production aircraft. After establishing a common industrial manufacturing program in which a large number of companies participated, led by the British company British Aerospace, the

The ECR version developed by Germany is equipped with sophisticated optical and electronic equipment for reconnaissance work, allowing it find out the exact position of enemy threats which can then be counteracted by its own systems, through the launch of HARM anti-radar missiles or with disruptive emissions.

German DASA and Italian Alenia, decided to establish a multi-national training center at the British Royal Air Force base in Cottesmore, the first aircraft destined for Germany and Great Britain flew on the 27th of July 1979. The first for Italy flew on the 25th of September 1981 because it had delayed production approval.

Production

Supplies to operational squadrons began in 1982 and in March 1986 Britain received an order to deliver a total of 24 aircraft to Saudi Arabia. Three months later an order was signed for the production of a seventh batch consisting of 124 aircraft.

In 1989, coinciding with the decision to improve the British GR1 units, the latest IDS production aircraft for Germany and Italy were delivered. In January 1992, the last of the German ECR's were ready and in November this same year production for the RAF finished. In 1993 an agreement was made to transfer 24 British ADV aircraft to Italy. A second order from Saudi Arabia arrived in 1993 for 48 units which were due to be delivered in 1998, a year in which the MLI (Mid Life Upgrade) process for German units would begin. This included a new avionics structure and new equipment associated with the Rafael laser designator pod, or the infra-red FLIR desig-

nator, and also including the modernization of Italian units if the budget allowed for it.

Take off

A total of 1,029 aircraft have been ordered including four presentation units some of which, since 1995, have been moved to the storage facility AMARC of the United States Air Force Davis-Monthan base in Arizona -as a result of the reduction of any threat.

The German Air Force operates 157 IDS aircraft, 55 training twin-seaters and 35 ECR's, shared out among squadrons stationed at no. 31 base at Norvenich, no.33 at Buchel, no.34 at Memmingen, no. 38 at Jever, no.51 at Schleswig/Jagel. Meanwhile the Navy incorporated 112 aircraft optimized for anti-ship attack, of which nearly half have

VERSIONS

MODEL	USER	IN SERVICE	MISSION
IDS	Germany, Italy, & Saudi Arabia	1982	All weather attack fighter bomber
IDS Navy	German Navy	1982	Anti-ship attack & zone reconnaissance
ECR	Germany & Italy	1990	Electronic warfare & reconnaissance
GR.1	Great Britain	1982	All weather attack fighter bomber
GR.1A	Great Britain	1987	All weather tactical reconnaissance
GR.4	Great Britain	1998	All weather attack fighter bomber optimized for night use
GR.4A	Great Britain	1999-2000	All weather tactical reconnaissance with capability for real time data transfer
ADV Mk3	Great Britain & Saudi Arabia	1986	All weather interceptor, aerial superiority fighter and combat patrol aircraft.

been transferred to the air force, grouped at Eggebeck Marinefliegergeshwader 2.

Italy obtained 88 IDS units and 12 twin-contro aircraft, 15 of which have been updated to the ECR version which allows them to launch AGM-88B Harm anti-radar missiles which were distributed among the 6th Stormo at the Brescia-Ghedi & Pratica de Mare bases. The 50th Stormo in Piacenza, and the 36th Stormo in Gioia del Colle, where anti-ship missions are carried out

with Kormoran missiles. The 24 ADV Mk3 units on a ten year lease are shared among the Gioia del Colle and the 37th Stormo in Trapani /Birgi.

Great Britain purchased 164 IDS aircraft, 14 for reconnaissance, 51 twin-control units, 173 ADV (24 transferred to Italy), which it shared out to, among others, the squadrons at the Bruggen base, Coningsby, Leeming and Leuchars with, in 1992, a detachment of four aircraft going to the Falkland Islands. For its part Saudi Arabia is in the process of incorporating 24 IDS units, 6 reconnaisance, 14 twin-seater twin-control trainers and 48 ADV aircraft which are being shared among the 7th and 66th Dahram squadrons.

Specializing

Flying at 540 knots and at an altitude of 200 feet or less, British Tornado formations began the attacks against Iraqi air bases on the night of the 17th of January 1991.

Armed with JP233 submunition launchers its mission was to destroy runways,

damage enemy aircraft and hit all kinds of vital systems making it impossible for the adversary to respond. This was the multi-national operation Desert Storm which punished Sadam Hussein.

With significant losses among the attackers due to the numbers of weapons and missile defensive systems, the Tornado IDS 's demonstrated that they were capable of carrying out the missions they were designed for with complete effectiveness, optimizing its possibilities by varying the wing angle as a result of the speed and flight altitude.

For attack and defence

The most advanced version of the IDS model is the British GR.4 which incorporates numerous equipment systems allowing it to demonstrate its combat effectiveness with employing radar which could reveal its presence. On the left side, just below the radar cone is the infra-red FLIR GEC TICM II system, and in the front seat the pilot is seated in a Martin-Baker Mk10, relying on a

> **VARIABLE WING ANGLE**
>
> With the wings fully swept back the Tornado improves its penetration capability at high speed, while with them fully extended the lift is increased.

holographic type Head Up Display (HUD) which allows images to be superimposed, as obtained by the FLIR. He has at his disposition modified avionics compatible with third generation night goggles, which now include a new multifunction display screen offering information on both digital flight maps and associated systems. He relies on the accuracy which new satellite positioning equipment (GPS) gives him for his navigation purposes.

The co-pilot, with the responsibility for managing the weaponry, has at his disposition two large data presentation screens and a cartographic visualization screen, allowing him to carry out his missions without problems. For his support he can rely on a GEC-Marconi TIALD laser designator with which he can launch guided bombs from a safe distance, and at the same time manage an electronic counter measure system activated by a Marconi Zeus radar warner.

The ADV version, in the process of being modernized, include subsystems such as the

CHARACTERISTICS

	IDS VERSION	ADV VERSION				
COST:	35 million dollars	42 million dollars	**Internal fuel load**	5,830 l		6,580 l
DIMENSIONS:			**External fuel load**	4,500 l		4,500 l
Length	16.70 m	18.1 m	**PROPULSION:**	Two jet engines		Two jet engines
Height	5.95 m	5.95 m		RB199-34R		RB199-34R
Wingspan				Mk103 with a unit		Mk104 with a unit
minimum	8.6 m	8.6 m		thrust of 6,750 kg.		thrust of 6,940 kg.
Wingspan			**PERFORMANCE:**			
maximum	13.91 m	13.91 m	**Ceiling service height**	15,000 m		15,000 m
Wing surface area	26.6 m²	26.6 m²	**Speed at high altitude**	Mach 2.2		Mach 2.2
WEIGHTS:			**Speed at low altitude**	Mach 1.22		Mach 1.22
Empty	13,890 kg	14,500 kg	**Runway length**	900 m		700 m
Maximum	27,950 kg	27,986 kg	**Combat range**	1,390 km		1,390 km
Maximum external load	9,000 kg	8,500 kg	**Extended range**	3,890 km		3,890 km
			Design load factor	+ 7.5 g's		+ 7.5 g's

AWS, ADMS and SPILS which optimize its working as an aerial defence aircraft and has been covered with absorbent sheets to reduce its radar signature. Operating with a Marconi Foxhunter Doppler radar which includes an IFF interrogator allowing it to detect its targets at a distance of 185 km. The pilot has responsibility for flight management while the co-pilot manages the air-to-air weaponry as well as the counter measure, interference and chaff equipment.

Offensive capability

With an external load capacity of 8 tonnes, the IDS version combines two 27 mm Mauser cannons with specific weapons such as MW-1 and JP233 submunition launchers; Paveway laser guided bombs; BL755 submunition bombs; Maverik laser guided bombs; Kormoran missiles; rocket launchers; free fall bombs; trusting in two Sidewinder AIM-9 missiles for self defence.

The ADV includes only one 27 mm cannon, the Sidewinders and four medium

INTERCEPTOR
ADV Tornados have been optimized for the interception of all kinds of aerial targets against which it can use Sky Flash radar guided air-to-air missiles.

DETAILS
A radar housed in the front nose; optimized air intakes for low altitude flight; in flight refueling capability; twin-seater cockpit provided advanced displays. These are some of the details of the Tornado (photograph to the left).

TAKE OFF
We can observe an IDS Italian Tornado on the ground at the Guedi air base, taxiing before carrying out a multi-national mission where it makes up a basic element of the Italian defence system (photograph to the right).

range Sky Flash missiles which in the future will be substituted by six Hughes AIM-120 AMRAAM's. Finally, this leaves it to be pointed out that normally electronic counter measure housings are installed, along with interference flare dispensers, Harm anti-radiation missiles and auxiliary fuel tanks.

Power

The attack version is equipped with two Turbo-Union RB199-34R jet engines, which in the Mk3 model produces 6,750 kg of thrust each, optimised to guarantee a flight without problems at low altitude where its automatic terrain following equipment, combining radar and inertial navigation , give it a high level of performance.

The model designated for aerial defence includes two Mk4 version jet engines with 6,940 kg of thrust each, while the electronic warfare ECR includes the Mk5 RB199 version which produces 10% more thrust than the initial model.

Designed to carry out landings and take offs vertically, thanks to vectorization of the jet engines exhaust gases. The Harrier presents outstanding features with the possibility of operating in multiple locations from large aircraft carriers to small clearings in a thick forest.

The creation of a military airplane

The idea of manufacturing a combat aircraft with vertical take off was developed in an era in which advances in the aeronautical world were the result of great interest in achieving greater and greater speed and capacity. Following this trend the British company Hawker Siddeley, in 1957, began the design of a military aircraft with the capability to land and take off on short

NAVY

Created to meet the specific requirements of the British Royal Navy, the Sea Harrier, which is also in service in India, has some differences to its multi-purpose brother, making it more effective in fleet air defence missions and surface target attack.

SPAIN

The AV-8B Harriers of the Spanish Navy are incorporated with the 9th Aircraft Fleet with approval to upgrade them to the Plus version around the end of the century.

strips of land. For this it collaborated with the company Bristol Engine, which specialized in high performance engines.

The Kestrel

After analyzing in detail the possibilities of project 1127, which managed to achieve the desired configuration, the initial proposal was tested in static flight at the end of September 1960, attached to the ground with steel cables. The good results obtained pushed the development, being followed with interest by Britain, the United States and Germany, who formed a tripartite squadron with nine P.1127 Kestrels.

After validating the concept and checking its possibilities the British Royal Air Force (RAF) designated the preproduction units it received as the Harrier and those which followed for ground attack and reconnaissance were identified by GR.Mk.1, being delivered from 1967.

Development

After configuring the T Mk2 model as a training twin-seater version (T for training), optimization work began in aspects such as improved propulsion plants which took the place of the Mk1A & Mk2A which were a part of the Pegasus 102. In 1971 the first aircraft arrived for the United States Marine Corps (USMC), which designated them as AV-8A Alfa and TAV-8A, and then shortly afterwards the British Mk3 & Mk4 versions entered service which included a

laser designator in an elongated radar dome and radar threat passive detector in the front upper part of the tail. Later it was supplied with a Pegasus 103 jet engine.

Coinciding with the process of improving the aircraft, in November 1972 one of these flew to the Gulf of Vizcaya where it performed an exhibition for the Spanish Navy, landing and taking off from the then helicopter carrier Matadora. The result of this was the purchase of 12 single and twin-seater model A aircraft- the Matador, which were maintained in service until 1997, when they were re-exported to Thailand.

The Harrier on board

Just as the Spanish marines did, the United States and Britain decided to incorporate the Harrier on its specialized ships. As such, while the marines were using the V-8A, the Royal Navy, which had been experimenting with the P.1127 on the aircraft carrier Ark Royal during February 1963, went on to secure a

naval version- the Sea Harrier..designated FRSI to carry out missions as a fighter and attack-reconnaissance aircraft. The first units were delivered in June 1979.

After participating successfully in the Falklands War in 1982, in which the different Harrier models deployed were responsible for two thirds of the one hundred Argentinean aircraft shot down, it was made clear that more advanced models

> **THAILAND**
> Thailand has incorporated ten Harrier AV-8A single and twin seaters with the aircraft carrier Chakri Naurebet, these aircraft belonging to the Spanish Navy until half way through 1996.

were needed. Although at the same time the success brought about the contract with the Indian Navy, in January 1983, for the delivery of a total of 23 Mk.51 Sea Harriers, destined for the aircraft carriers Viraat and Vikrant.

An advanced aircraft

In 1984 deliveries of the McDonnell Douglas AV-8B Bravo and TAV-8B to the USMC began, with redesigned wings, greater weapon carrying capacity, more powerful engines. Advanced cockpit and a designator in the nose for launching precision bombs. 12 were incorporated by Spain in 1987 and adopted in the same year, as the Mk.5, by the RAF. In parallel to earlier deliveries the performance of the Night Attack prototype were evaluated. Adapted for night time combat thanks to the use of an infra-red sensor. The results were so good that the marines quickly decided to adopt it and the British began the transformation of their Mk.5 to this version, known as the Mk.7.

> **GR7**
> Manufactured by the British company British Aerospace, the GR7 is the most advanced version equipping the British Royal Air Force and is capable of carrying out attack missions both day and night. The pilot can be helped here by third generation night vision goggles or with the Infra-red FLIR tracker which supplies accurate images of the target.

With the operational possibilities coming to an end in 1990, the modernization of the British Sea Harrier to the F/A2 model was begun, incorporating a new GEC-Marconi Blue Vixen radar; with the fuselage lengthened by 35 cm; an integrated redesigned weaponry system and improved cockpit. Shortly after, the Americans, Spanish and Italians applied for the production and incorporation of the AV-8B Plus equipped with the Hughes AN/APG-65 radar; more powerful engines; decoy flare launchers in the upper and lower part of the fuselage; the cockpit modified with new display screens. The deliveries began in 1993, and also included a wide program of updating for the B series to the new standard in a process which will be finished at the beginning of the 21st century.

The Plus

Operating from air bases, eventual air fields, amphibious boats or small aircraft carriers, the Harrier has demonstrated its capability of carrying out multi-purpose missions, with few differences between those units manufactured in the United States and those built in Great Britain.

The propulsion

The use of a Rolls Royce F402-RR-408 Pegasus 11-6 jet engine, producing 9,000 kg of thrust and including four engine flow deflectors located in pairs on both sides of the fuselage, permits these aircraft to perform in multiple scenarios. A rotary type which the pilot controls within normal limits, allows the escape gases to be directed, giving the possibility of vertical take off and landing, or the execution of agile maneuveres during close aerial combat missions.

Configuration

Designed for a useful life of 6,000 hours, the aircraft fuselage incorporate small differences with respect to other designs such as sturdy wings produced from carbon fiber composite materials, giving increased lift and greater capacity to carry fuel. Central fins replace the cannon housing when it is not being used. Large inlet nozzles improve the cruising speed and optimize the short lan-

---

PLUS

Designed to form a part of the Marine Corps and the Spanish & Italian Navies, the Harrier AV-8B+ presents greater potential than other earlier designs, relying on the multi-purpose Hughes AN/APG-65 radar, including an advanced cockpit, repowered engines and structural modifications to achieve better performance.

LOAD

With four fixing on each of the wings and fuselage, the GR7 can carry a wide range of weapons and support equipment for its combat missions.

---

ding and take off capabilities positioning of the support wheels in the wings which help the landing operation, with additional front and rear under carriages the inclusion of extended leading edges to improve the turning capability during air-to-air combat; the absence of rear nozzles, relying on the lateral deflectors.

Equipment

Sitting in a Martin Baker or UPC/Sentel ejector seat, the pilot has at his disposition an advanced cockpit which includes multifunction display screens and instrumentation appropriate to the missions.

It controls the air space and approaching land with an advanced multi-mode

WEAPONRY

AIR TO AIR MISSIONS	AIR TO SURFACE MISSIONS
A five barrel 25 mm GE GAU-12/U cannon or two 30 or 25 mm Royal Ordance Aden cannons. AIM-9L/M Sidewinder missiles and AIM-120 AMRAAM guides missiles.	Rocket launchers; general use bombs; BL 755 submunition bombs; Paveway laser guided bombs; multi-purpose AGM-65E Maverik missiles. The Hapoon anti-ship missile significant for its weight.

Doppler Hughes AN/APG-65 radar which is also the F-18 Hornet, and is able to launch its weapons accurately with the help of an infra-red illuminator; this model is equipped with a Smiths Industries HUD/HDD; instrumentation compatible with night vision goggles; a high precision inertial navigator; communication equipment resistant to electronic counter measures; a digital color map display; complete self defence equipment with interference cartridge launchers; advanced disruption system and a threat signaling display.

AV-8B PLUS TECHNICAL CHARACTERISTICS

COST:	50 million dollars	Internal fuel load	4,600 l
DIMENSIONS:		External fuel load	4,800 l
Length	14.55 m	PERFORMANCE:	
Height	3.55 m	High altitude speed	Mach 0.98
Wingspan	9.25 m	Low altitude speed	Mach 0.87
Wing surface area	21.37 m²	Combat range	259 km/h
WEIGHTS:			1,100 km/h
Empty	6,740 kg	Extended range	3,641 km
Maximum	14,061 kg	Design load factor	7 g's
Maximum external load	6,000 kg		

SUPPORTS

On each wing, supports are fitted for extra fuel tanks, and to carry the different types weapons necessary for executing missions.

HOUSINGS

The «Harrier A» is able to take advantage of auxiliary fuel tanks. Though in place of fuel tanks, containers carrying supplies for ground forces can also be fitted here.

AIRBRAKES

There is a large hydraulic air brake in the central part of the fuselage, this helps to reduce speed and makes the aircraft more maneuverable. A Tracor decoy flare launcher, firing infrared canisters to confuse the tracking missilesand canisters of multi-band CHAFF to disrupt enemy radar are also fitted.

FUSELAGE

The upper part of the fuselage incorporates various dynamic air intakes, which cool the internal electronic systems and engine exhaust nozzles. In addition there are markings and identification lights when flying in formation at right.

DIGITAL

The cockpits in the «Plus» variant, have incorporated notable improvements, including the management of the data presentation, with three multi-functionary digital screens, and a new Head Up Display (HUD). The improvements help the pilot to perform his mission more effectively, and make the likelihood of his mission being successful, a certainty.

REFUELING

Incorporated on the left side of the fuselage is the in-flight refueling nozzle which extends to receive fuel from a tanker aircraft, and is then retracted so that it doesn't effect the aerodynamics . With this process the mission range is significantly increased.

PEGASUS

Original in its design and configuration, the Harrier's Pegasus jet engine is distinguished from most other engines by its physical size, and by the size of the inlet duct. It is fitted with two swivel nozzle's which enable the pilot to direct the jet exhaust in almost any direction he requires. With this unique feature he is able to take off and land vertically.

LANDING CARRIAGE

Strongly built so that it can withstand heavy landing impacts, the undercarriage is fitted with a double wheel at the back to improve taxiing, It is also set back somewhat to allow it to be retracted into the fuselage.

The television images obtained during the Gulf War went around the world. With these images, it could be appreciated, with complete clarity, the effects of guided weapons attacking surface targets such as bunkers, aircraft hangers, arms depots, communication centres etc, making it clear what modern systems are capable of if used properly.

Necessity

When airplanes went to war they were thought of as little more than observation platforms. However it wasn't long before they were being used to bomb troops with hand bombs and grenades. This evolution continued with newer, more capable and specialized aircraft being developed, such as those used in the Second World War. Though it wasn't until the Vietnam War that air capability advanced to the exent that attacks on all types of targets could be carried out in

almost any kind of weather. This included the first use of precision-guided weapons to destroy bridges, which allowed the *Vietcong* to maintain its supply routes.

This evolution has continued until the present day where it has been demonstrated both in the Falklands conflict and the Gulf War that air power is essential if you wish to maintain complete superiority.

Quick shot

Used by the majority of fighter bombers and occasionally fitted to training and transport aircraft, you can find the housings for

these light machine guns and cannons incorporated in the fuselage of the iarcraft.

Light machine guns normally have a cliber of 7.62 x 51 mm (the 0.308 Winchester for instance), though in some instance they do have a larger caliber of 12.7 x 99 mm. The cannon is an instrinsic part of virtually every combat aircraft, it is fitted to most fighter bombers as one of their basic components. Of the many models on the market, particularly noteworthy are the multi-barrel United States Vulcan 20 & 30 mm cannons and the 27 mm German cannon, together with the Swiss, Russian and French 30 mm cannon.

The United States relies on high rates of

AIR TO SURFACE WEAPONS CAPABILITY

WEAPON	OBJECTIVE
Cannon, usually 20,27 or 30 mm	These can attack lightly protected vehicles such as lorry convoys, lightly armoured vehicles, fuel tanks, control centers.
Rockets	Employed in salvos with the possibility of saturating a wide area with considerable effects against lightly protected troops or vehicles
Submunition dispensers	These launch small bombs or mines with anti-removal mechanisms to cause multiple impacts in a determined area and they are useful against lightly protected objectives or to brake the advance of ground troops.
Free-fall bombs	Normally, 125 to 1,000 kg, incorporating an explosive charge in a metal body sufficient to hit lightly protected targets.
Anti-runway bombs	Designed to damage runways and impede enemy reaction.
Guided bombs	Working with laser illuminators or optical tracking aircraft, they incorporate a guided warhead which allows it to hit targets with such precision that it is possible to bring them through a 1.5x1.5 meter window.
Guided missiles	Working with the carrier aircraft's radar, infra-red or television equipment, they have an intermediate range and can destroy targets which require high precision, such as bridges, shelters, ships etc.
Anti-radar missiles	Locating detector radar emissions, and fixing on the waves emitted, guided until hitting or destroying the radar or associated anti-aircraft missile launchers.
Anti-ship missiles	With its own self guidance system it can hit ships sailing at a radius of 100 km, one of these being capable of sinking a 4,000 ton ship.
Nuclear weapons	Usually for tactical use, combining missiles and free-fall bombs with atomic warheads of limited power, sufficient to delay the enemy's advance or destroy very important targets.

subwing fixings in the French DEFA model, used by Spanish Mirage F-1 aircraft, increasing the capability of the single-seat aircraft, and allowing the twin-seat aircraft to carry out complementary missions.

In addition to machine guns and cannons, 68 or 70 mm rockets maybe carried to use on secondary missions. These again are carried on under wing fixtures or on the underside of the fuselage, and can be fired individually or in salvos.

Free-fall & sub-munitions

Free-fall bombs are constructed in a traditional way, which has not varied substantially in the last fifty years. The body is normally made from cast iron and has a more or less aerodynamic shape. The explosive, which can vary in composition and weight depending on the nature of the target, fills the interior of the bomb. Stabilizing fins are fitted to the back of the bomb so that it remains stable as it drops through the air. Before the bomb is loaded onto the aircraft, a weapons specialist, who is member of the ground crew, fits a fuse to the nose of the bomb.

Most conventional bombs fall into the following categories: Those that free-fall after being released from the aircraft, and are as described above, bombs similar to the free- fall types, which are fitted with a parachute or other mechanical retarding device in its tail cone to delay it reaching the target long enough to allow the attacking aircraft time to leave the immediate area, those fitted with a decelerating rocket, which fire just before impact to achieve maximum penetration and destruction and special ground-piercing bombs that destroy aircraft runways and roads around bases. In addition there are incendiary bombs which contain highly combustible liquids and chemicals, air

fire of some 6,000 rounds per minute to achieve saturation and destruction of a target. This requires a complex system of ammunition supply with magazines of 500 rounds to ensure that there are enough rounds when the aircraft is on a mission. Meanwhile the Europeans and Russians who normally it one or two in the aircraft's fuselage, rely on the multi-purpose nature of their munitions and the accuracy to destroy their targets. For example, different versions are mounted on

BRAKE BOMBS

A parachute braking system attached to the free-fall bomb allows a time delay from the launch until the impact, allowing the launch aircraft to leave the zone without suffering from the effects of the explosion which could be the case with launches at very low altitude.

detonation bombs, which have an enormous destructive effect on the area around the detonation and cluster bombs, which also explode in mid air and discharges different kinds of sub-munitions as they do.

Suspended from sub-wing supports during flight and with a weight normally around 125 to 1,000 kg, there are countless numbers and types of bombs in many countries. The most famous and most copied are the Mk family of the United States. In addition there is the Egyptian Kadar, ad the Spanish «Expal» together with its many versions. The French Durandal, BAP & BL, the Yugoslav FAB, the Chilean WB, Iraqi KAAKAA; and the Russian Betab & AO/AOkh. A different type is the United States 6,800 kg BLU-82 bomb which is carried in a MC-130H Hercules. These were used two at a time during the Gulf War to clear routes through minefields. These bombs are capable of making a breach in a minefield of some two kilometers in radius.

In the case of sub-munitions, these are normally used as normal bombs or they can be delivered to the target by a missile. Sub-munitions are small explosive bombs, mines, or other special devices, which are dispersed over an area to cause a large amount of

ROCKET LAUNCHERS
The canisters for 70mm rockets allow them to be fired in an individual or salvo mode. They are very effective in attacking unprotected troops and light vehicles. At the same time their cost is low, making them affordable for any country.

success lies in the large amount of small explosive charges the bomb or missile contains. Among the many examples available, those which are most prominent are the British Damocles & BL755, French BLG66, German MW-1, United States CBU's & JSOW, Chilean CB, Russian KMG-U, South African CB470 and Spanish BME 330.

damage to targets such as a mechanized columns, air bases or to brake up offensives by ground troops sand mobile forces.

Its immediate military effect is limited because of its small explosive charge, but its

GULF WAR
The French Air Force employed its Jaguar attack aircraft to attack specific targets in Iraq, missions in which the 400 kg BGL bombs were very useful. A laser contained within the pod under the fuselage guides the bomb.

Guided bombs

The Americans began using laser-guided or electro-optically guided bombs in 1967 during the Vietnam conflict, demonstrating their ability to regularly hit, with great precision, targets such as bridge columns and key points in the Hanoi-Haifong area.

With the system validated and maintained up to the present day, but now with far more advanced and accurate examples, the system consists of installing a guidance head in the

(Global Positioning System) receiver, which monitors the weapons position as it heads towards its pre-determined target, and makes any nesessary corrections to ensure the bomb impacts on its target. It can cover distances of around 10 km and has an accuracy of 10 meters. Another interesting development is the South African BARF (Booster Anti Radar Bomb) which consists of a Mk82 250 kg bomb provided with a tracker using a passive radar and a system of moveable fins to direct it to the target.

nose of the bomb and providing its fins with a flight control system. The target can be illuminated by an operator in the aircraft's rear seat, using a ground signaler/infiltrator or by independent equipment housed in another aircraft. The bomb captures the signal reflected from the target and follows it until hitting the desired impact point, which could be as small as a building window. In the case of bombs being guided by electo-optical guidance systems, these require good atmospheric conditions before being used. The guidance system can be substituted by a tracker, which follows the optical contrast of the impact point being marked by the operator.

At the moment there are a number of these bombs being produced, among which include the American BLU-109/B, the French 400 &1,000 kg LGB, the Israeli Griffin, Pyramid & Guillotine, the Russian KAB and the American Paveway III family of GBU-24,27 & 28.

At the same time other guidance possibilities are being tested such as the American MK-82 GPS Guided «Taikit» and MK-84 GATS/GAM. These weapons include a GPS

ADVANCED
Russian industry has recently shown its multipurpose and advanced X-31A missile, with a range of some 100 km. It which can be used in missions against surface ships and to attack surface-to-air missile sites and associated guidance systems.

SLAM
Developed from the anti-ship Harpoon and the multipurpose Maverik, the SLAM is an independently guided weapon with great accuracy, able to attack both surface targets and ships in port, causing significant damage with its 500 pound explosive warhead.

CANNONS
For secondary use, all modern fighter bombers have one or two cannons with a variable caliber of between 20 & 30mm, allowing the firing of many kinds of munition at a high rate of fire, destroying lightly protected targets.

MAVERIK AGM-65 MISSILES

Platform	Aircraft : F-4,F-16F-18,AV-8B, JAS-39, P-3 Helicopter : AH-1W, SH-2G
Models	- AGM-65A, B & H guided by television with electro-optical auto-guidance - AGM-65D, G & F guided by infra-red auto-guidance from captured thermal energy. - AGM-65E guided by laser illumination - AGM-65IR operational prototype for anti-ship use
Explosive charge	Conical type & 55 kg for the A,B & D versions. Fragmentation/penetration, 125 kg, for the E, F & G versions.
Fuse	Impact, Proximity and Delayed to allow it to explode after penetrating the target.
Effectiveness	5,500 of these were launched in the Gulf War, obtaining a success rate of 92%.
Users	The United States, France, Spain, Australia, Germany, Egypt, Greece, Iran, Israel, Saudi Arabia, Morocco, Sweden, Switzerland, Singapore, South Korea, Turkey, Taiwan etc.

Specialized missiles

A wide range of missiles exist that are designed to carry out single purpose or multipurpose tasks. They are prepared for attacking specific targets within a millimeter of accuracy, or for attacking naval targets and enemy radar sites and neutralizing them. For this reason each model incorporates an explosive warhead which can be adapted for any purpose that might be required. The propulsion system must be able to carry enough fuel so that it can reach its target, which can be any where from a 100 km in most cases to many to hundreds of kilometers in the case of cruise missiles. The guidance system must also have the capability of finding its way to the target and at the same time is able to discern between one target and another.

Among those in use at present are the AGM Maverik, Harpoon Block II which has a submunitions warhead, the United States SLAM & SLAMER, The Argentinean Martin

MAVERIK

Guided by television, laser or infrared, the multipurpose Maverik missile can be used by aircraft and helicopters to attack many kinds of surface targets, including ships at sea, with a probability of success greater than 90 %.

THE GULF WAR

The United States AGM-65 Maverik Missile was widely used to attack Iraqi surface targets during the Gulf War, demonstrating a high level of reliability and hitting the majority of designated targets.

GUIDED BOMBS

The accuracy of guided bombs comes from the inclusion of a tracking head which follows the signal emitted by a system illuminating the target, marking the exact point of impact. These are very useful for attacking all kinds of fixed targets.

Pescador, the Swiss RB05, the French AS 30L and AS-7 Kerry, the Russian AS-10 Karen & AS-14 Kedge, the outstanding German anti-ship Kormoran 2, the British Sea Eagle & Sea Kua, the Israeli Gabriel, the French Exocet- this missile caused devastation with the British fleet during the Falklands War and hit a United States frigate while it was patrolling in the Persian Gulf, causing serious damage; the United States AGM-84 Harpoon, the Swedish

RBS 15, the Norwegian AGM-119 Penguin, the Russian X-15C, X-31 & X-35, and the Italian Marte 2. With regards to anti-radar missiles there are the British ALARM, the French Martel, the South African BARB, the Russian AS-9 & X-25M and the United States AGM-88 Harm (High Speed Anti-Radiation Missile).

The Nuclear Option

Nuclear bombs and various other kinds of missiles with atomic warheads can be used both tactically and strategically in the modern battlefield. Among these bombs are the United States B61 & B83, and with respect to missiles, the French ASMP, different United States cruise missiles together with the advanced Russian models.